"Seasoned by personal wit, shaped by years of pastoral ministry, and highly skilled in interpreting God's Word, Kevin DeYoung is the right person to write this book. DeYoung fleshes out the Ten Commandments in a way that helps us see the wisdom of our Creator and Redeemer in directing us on our pilgrim way. I highly recommend this book!"

Michael Horton, J. Gresham Machen Professor of Systematic Theology and Apologetics, Westminster Seminary California; Host, *White Horse Inn*; author, *Core Christianity*

THE 10 COMMANDMENTS

THE 10 COMMANDMENTS

What They Mean, Why They Matter,
and Why We Should Obey Them

Kevin DeYoung

WHEATON, ILLINOIS

Library of Congress Cataloging-in-Publication Data

Names: DeYoung, Kevin, author.
Title: The Ten Commandments : what they mean, why they matter, and why we should obey them / Kevin DeYoung.
Description: Wheaton : Crossway, 2018. | Includes bibliographical references and index.
Identifiers: LCCN 2018011864 (print) | LCCN 2018029548 (ebook) | ISBN 9781433559686 (pdf) | ISBN 9781433559693 (mobi) | ISBN 9781433559709 (epub) | ISBN 9781433559679 (hc)
Subjects: LCSH: Ten commandments--Criticism, interpretation, etc.
Classification: LCC BS1285.52 (ebook) | LCC BS1285.52 .D49 2018 (print) | DDC 241.5/2--dc23
LC record available at https://lccn.loc.gov/2018011864

Crossway is a publishing ministry of Good News Publishers.

LB		28	27	26	25	24	23	22	21	20	19	18
15	14	13	12	11	10	9	8	7	6	5	4	3	2	1

To Roy and Barbara Bebee
Wonderful in-laws, loving grandparents, faithful Christians

Contents

Introduction

The Good News of Law

And God spoke all these words, saying, "I am the LORD your God, who brought you out of the land of Egypt, out of the house of slavery."

Exodus 20:1–2

Exodus 20:1–2 introduces one of the most famous sections in the Bible—indeed, one of the most important pieces of religious literature in the whole world—the Ten Commandments. Oddly enough, they are never actually called the Ten Commandments. The Hebrew expression, which occurs three times in the Old Testament (Ex. 34:28; Deut. 4:13; 10:4), literally means "ten words." This is why Exodus 20 is often referred to as the Decalogue, *deka* being the Greek word for "ten" and *logos* meaning "word." These are the Ten Words that God gave the Israelites at Mount Sinai—and, I'll argue, the Ten Words that God wants all of us to follow.

Whatever we call them, the Ten Commandments are certainly commands—more than that for sure, but not less. The problem people have is not with what they're called but with what they contain. Studying the Ten Commandments reveals the very heart of human rebellion: we don't like God telling us what we can and cannot do.

The Noncommandment Commandments

A few years ago there was an article on the CNN website entitled, "Behold, Atheists' New Ten Commandments."[1] The story explains how Lex Bayer, an executive at AirBnB, and John Figdor, a humanist chaplain at Stanford University, tried to crowdsource ten "non-commandments." They solicited input from around the world and offered ten thousand dollars to the winning would-be Moseses. After receiving more than 2,800 submissions, they appointed a panel of thirteen judges to select the ten winners. Here's what they came up with, the ten noncommandments of our age:

1. Be open-minded and be willing to alter your beliefs with new evidence.
2. Strive to understand what is most likely to be true, not to believe what you wish to be true.
3. The scientific method is the most reliable way of understanding the natural world.
4. Every person has the right to control of [*sic*] their body.
5. God is not necessary to be a good person or to live a full and meaningful life.
6. Be mindful of the consequences of all your actions and recognize that you must take responsibility for them.
7. Treat others as you would want them to treat you, and can reasonably expect them to want to be treated. Think about their perspective.
8. We have the responsibility to consider others, including future generations.
9. There is no one right way to live.
10. Leave the world a better place than you found it.

That sounds about right—not with respect to God's law, but in terms of how many people think of their moral obligations. These ten noncommandments perfectly capture the default moral code at the front end of the twenty-first century.

Nevertheless, I would hope, perhaps naively, that after a few moments of reflection, we would see that these new commandments are filled with some stunning contradictions. They say you don't need God to be a good person or to know how to live (#5), and yet the seventh noncommandment is a summary of the Golden Rule, which came from Jesus (Matt. 7:12). They talk about the scientific method (#3), without an awareness that Francis Bacon's method of inductive observation gained popularity in North America in large measure because of Presbyterian and Reformed theologians who saw Bacon's approach as a good way to make observations about God's created world.

More to the point, these noncommandments are logically indefensible. They're presumably called "noncommandments" so as not to sound so commandment-ish. Yet they're all commands! They all carry the force of a moral *ought*. We live in a paradoxical age where many will say, "Right and wrong is what you decide for yourself," and yet these same people will rebuke others for violating any number of assumed commands. As a culture, we may be quite free and liberal when it comes to sex, but we can be absolutely fundamentalist when it comes to the moral claims of the sexual revolution. The old swear words may not scandalize us any longer, but now there are other words—offensive slurs and insults—that will quickly put someone out of polite company. We are still a society with a moral code.

And then there's the second to last of these noncommandments. How does this *ought* square with the other nine in the list? How can we be told to leave the planet a better place and think of others and exercise control over our bodies if there really is "no one right way to live"? Which is it: do as we say or do as you please? It can't be both.

I know the contest was a publicity stunt for a book Bayer and Figdor wrote on being atheistic humanists, but the authors seem to genuinely believe it's a fine idea to develop your moral code by taking the temperature of those around you. Elsewhere in the CNN article we read:

> Bayer said humans are hardwired for compassion, and the scientific method and wisdom of crowds—or the tribes that gather online each day—will weed out bad ideas. In other words, this is an open-ended, and hopefully progressive, process, he said.[2]

I don't know what Internet they're looking at, but I have not found "online" to be a place that's entirely trustworthy for weeding out bad ideas. Remember, Bayer and Figdor had to appoint a committee of thirteen judges to pick out the best non-commandments. They realized instinctively that we might not come up with a great moral code just by asking people what they think.

In fact, going to the Internet to find your way in the world is often one of the worst ideas. Not too long ago I came across a story about the British government's attempt to name a $287 million polar research vessel. In an effort to generate publicity for the new vessel, the government decided to name the royal research ship by way of an Internet vote. The agency in charge of the contest suggested to British citizens that they look at names such as Ernest Shackleton (the famous explorer), Endeavor, or Falcon. But the people's overwhelming, runaway choice for this state-of-the-art research vessel—the clear winner of the Internet vote—was (are you ready for it?): "Boaty McBoatface." You've got to love the British sense of humor, but that wasn't exactly the name officials were hoping for. In the end, the agency decided not to go with the clear winner of the contest and instead picked the fourth-place entry, naming the boat after Sir David Attenborough.[3] The wisdom of crowds isn't always wise.

And that goes for commandments as well as for boats. The Bible says the fear of the Lord is the beginning of wisdom (Prov. 9:10). The way to find moral instruction is not by listening to your gut but by listening to God. If we want to know right from wrong, if we want to know how to live the good life, if we want to know how to live in a way that blesses our friends and neighbors, we'd be wise to do things God's way, which means paying careful attention to the Ten Commandments.

———

Before we look at the commandments themselves, we need to lay some important groundwork. In particular, there are two questions that need to be answered:

1. Why should we study the Ten Commandments?
2. Why should we obey the Ten Commandments?

Let me give you five answers to each question. Think of it as ten words before the Ten Words.

Why Should We Study the Ten Commandments?

The answer to this first question used to be self-evident. Everyone just *knew*—whether Christian or not—that the Ten Commandments are important. But now, even inside the church, there can be a deep disinterest, or even a dis-ease, about spending a lot of time on the Bible's moral code. We need to be convinced all over again that the Ten Commandments matter and deserve our careful attention. Here are five reasons why.

Reason 1: General Ignorance

First, most people are simply ignorant of the Ten Commandments. Fewer and fewer churches read the Ten Commandments in worship. Children are not made to memorize the Decalogue anymore. It would probably be embarrassing for both children and adults if we randomly picked people on a Sunday morning to come up front and recite the Ten Commandments.

And if ignorance is a danger in the church, it's almost a certainty outside the church. A recent survey found that only 14 percent of Americans could name the Ten Commandments. By comparison, a quarter of all Americans can name the seven ingredients in a Big Mac, nearly three out of four can name all three stooges, and more than one in three know all six kids from the Brady Bunch, a television show that was cancelled before I was born! More of us know that a Big Mac has two all-beef patties than know that "You shall not murder" is one of the Ten Commandments.[4]

It's no exaggeration to say that these Ten Words handed down at Mount Sinai have been the most influential law code ever given. That's why you'll find Moses or the Ten Commandments (admittedly, among other symbols and other lawgivers) in at least three different architectural embellishments in the United States Supreme Court building. "Keep them and do them, for that will be your wisdom and your understanding in the sight of the peoples, who, when they hear all these statutes, will say, 'Surely this great nation is a wise and understanding people'" (Deut. 4:6). That has proven to be true. The commandments given to the nation of Israel, as recorded in the Scriptures, have become known all throughout the world. Whether we think they're right or not, simply out of an interest in world history—especially Western history—we should not be ignorant of them.

Reason 2: Historical Instruction

The church has historically put the Ten Commandments at the center of its teaching ministry, especially for children and new believers. For centuries, catechetical instruction was based on three things: the Apostles' Creed, the Lord's Prayer, and the Ten Commandments. In other words, when people asked, "How do we do discipleship? How do we teach our kids about the Bible? What do new Christians need to know about Christianity?" their answers always included an emphasis on the Ten Commandments. In the Heidelberg Catechism, for example, eleven of the fifty-two Lord's Days focus on the Ten Commandments. The same is true in forty-two of the 107 questions in the Westminster Shorter Catechism, in more than half of the Lutheran Large Catechism, and in 120 out of 750 pages of the Catechism of the Catholic Church. Across various traditions, there has been a historic emphasis on the Ten Commandments.

Reason 3: Centrality to Mosaic Ethics

The Ten Commandments are central to the ethics of the Mosaic covenant. We see this right from the prologue. There's an important change in Exodus at the beginning of chapter 20. The Lord is no longer telling Moses to go down and relay a message to the people. That's how the Lord operated in chapter 19, but now in chapter 20 God is speaking "all these words" (v. 1) directly to the Israelites. That's why, at the end of the Ten Commandments, the people cry out to Moses, "You speak to us, and we will listen; but do not let God speak to us, lest we die" (Ex. 20:19). They were too terrified to have God speak to them without a mediator, which says something about the stunning display of God's power in chapters 19 and 20 and underlines the importance of the Decalogue.

Moreover, the language in verse 2 is a deliberate echo of God's call to Abraham. Look at the similarities:

I am the LORD who brought you out from Ur of the Chaldeans. (Gen. 15:7)

I am the LORD your God, who brought you out of the land of Egypt. (Ex. 20:2)

At these great epochal moments in redemptive history—first with Abraham, and now with Moses and the people of Israel at the foot of Mount Sinai—God says, in effect, "I am the Lord who brought you out of this strange land to be your God and to give you this special word."

Some people—including a number of good Old Testament scholars—will say, "Well, look, there are all sorts of commandments. The Ten Commandments are succinct, and they've played an important role in the history of the church, but they're simply the introduction to the Mosaic law. There are hundreds of statutes in the Pentateuch, and the Bible never says these ten are in a class all by themselves." While it's true that the Bible doesn't say to print the Ten Commandments in boldface, we shouldn't undersell their special stature in ancient Israel. They came from God as he spoke to the people face-to-face (Deut. 5:1–5), and they came from Mount Sinai amidst fire, cloud, thick darkness, and a loud voice (Deut. 5:22–27). Exodus 20 marks a literal and spiritual high point in the life of Israel. It's no wonder the tablets of the law, along with the manna and Aaron's staff, were placed inside the ark of the covenant (Heb. 9:4).

There are going to be many more laws in the Old Testament. But these first ten are foundational for the rest. The Ten Commandments are like the constitution for Israel, and what follows are the regulatory statutes. The giving of the law changes sharply from chapter 20 to chapters 21 and 22. The Ten Commandments are clear, definite, absolute standards of right and wrong. Once you get to chapter 21, we shift to application. You can see the distinctive language leading off each paragraph in chapters 21 and 22: words such as "when," "whoever," and "if." This is the case law meant to apply the constitutional provisions carved in stone on Mount Sinai. From the very outset of Israel's formal existence as a nation, the Ten Commandments had a special place in establishing the rules for their life together.

Reason 4: Centrality to New Testament Ethics

The Ten Commandments are also central to the ethics of the New Testament. Think of Mark 10:17, for example. This is where the rich young ruler comes to Jesus and asks, "What must I do to inherit eternal life?" Jesus says to him, "You know the commandments." Then he lists the second table of the law, the commandments that relate to our neighbors: "Do not murder, Do not commit adultery, Do not steal, Do not bear false witness, Do not defraud, Honor your father and mother" (v. 19). Jesus isn't laying out a path for earning eternal life. We know from the rest of the story that Jesus is setting the young man up for a fall, because the one command he obviously hasn't obeyed is the one command Jesus skips—Do not covet (vv. 20–22). But it is noteworthy that when Jesus has to give a convenient summary of our neighborly duties, he goes straight to the Ten Commandments.

We see something similar in Romans 13. When the apostle Paul wants to give a summary of what it means to be a Christian living in obedience to God, he looks to the Ten Commandments:

> Owe no one anything, except to love each other, for the one who loves another has fulfilled the law. For the commandments, "You shall not commit adultery, You shall not murder, You shall not steal, You shall not covet," and any other commandment, are summed up in this word: "You shall love your neighbor as yourself." (Rom. 13:8–9)

Paul says, much like Jesus did, that the Ten Commandments are the way for God's people to love one another. When we love, we fulfill the commandments, and when we obey the commandments, we are fulfilling the law of love.

Paul does something similar in 1 Timothy 1. After establishing that the law is good if one uses it lawfully (v. 8), Paul proceeds in verses 9 and 10 to rattle through the second table of the law, referring to the wicked "who strike their fathers and mothers" (a violation of the fifth commandment), and "murderers" (a violation of the sixth commandment), and the sexually immoral and men who practice homosexuality (violations of the seventh commandment), and "enslavers" (a violation of the eighth commandment), and liars and perjurers (violations of the ninth commandment). Again, when Paul needs a recognizable way to summarize ethical instruction for the people of God, he goes back to the Ten Commandments.

By Jewish tradition, there are 613 laws in the Pentateuch. They all matter because they all teach us something about love for God and neighbor. But the 613 can be summarized by the Ten Commandments, which can in turn be summarized by two: love the Lord your God with all your heart, soul, and mind, and love your neighbor as yourself (see Matt. 22:37–40). Jesus certainly transforms the Ten Commandments, as we will see, but he never meant to abolish them (Matt. 5:17).

As we go through these studies, we will find that the law drives us to our knees, shows us our sin, and leads us to the cross. We need forgiveness. None of us keeps these commands perfectly. At the same time, however, for those who have been forgiven and know Christ, we see in both the Old and New Testaments that the Ten Commandments are foundational for living an obedient life pleasing to God.

Reason 5: The Law Is Good

Finally, we ought to study the Decalogue because the commandments are good. How strange, we think, that the psalmist should say that his delight is in the law of the Lord (Ps. 1:2). We can understand delighting in God's love or his grace or his promises, but in his law? Who loves commandments? Well, the psalmist does. He understands that God lays down his law for our good, not for our groaning. The good news of law, C. S. Lewis once remarked, is like the good news of arriving on solid ground after a shortcut gone awry through the mud, muck, and mire. After fumbling about in the squishy, stinky mess, you're relieved to finally hit something solid, something you can trust, something you can count on.

Have you ever thought about how much better life would be if everyone kept the Ten Commandments? We may grumble about rules and regulations, but think of what an amazing place the world would be if these ten rules were obeyed. If everyone kept the Ten Commandments, we wouldn't need copyright laws, patent laws, or intellectual property rights. We wouldn't need locks on our doors or fraud protection. We wouldn't have to spend money on weapons and defense systems. We wouldn't need courts, contracts, or prisons. Can you imagine what life would be like if people obeyed the Ten Commandments? The law is not an ugly thing; it is good and righteous and holy (Rom. 7:12).

Five Reasons to Obey the Ten Commandments

The Ten Commandments are not to be ignored. It's important that we study and understand them. But, of course, it's more important that we obey them. God isn't impressed by an intellectually careful analysis that puts the Decalogue at the center of Christian discipleship. He expects disciples to actually follow these commands.

But for the right reasons. Working hard to obey the Ten Commandments from the wrong motivation and for the wrong end is a surefire way to live out our relationship with God in the wrong way. God gave the commandments that they might be obeyed—not to earn salvation but because of who we are, who God is in himself, who he is to us, where we are, and what he has done.

Reason 1: Who We Are

Don't miss the obvious: Exodus 19 comes before Exodus 20. God has already identified the Israelites as "a kingdom of priests and a holy nation" (Ex. 19:6). They are a people set apart. The same is true of us. As Christians, we too are a kingdom of priests and a holy nation (1 Pet. 2:9). We must be prepared to stand alone, to look different, and to have rules the world doesn't understand. Of course, we aren't always the holy people we should be, but that's what he has called us to be. That's who we are. We are God's people, set apart to live according to God's ways.

Reason 2: Who God Is in Himself

The opening verses in Exodus 20 are not just filler before the commandments start rolling. They establish who God is and why we should obey him. In verse 2 God reveals himself again as "the Lord," that is, as Yahweh their covenant-keeping God. This is the God who spoke to Moses in the burning bush. This is the God who said, "I am who I am" (Ex. 3:14). This is the sovereign, self-existent, self-sufficient, almighty creator God. This is the God of the plagues and the Red Sea and the manna in the wilderness. This is not a God to be trifled with. If there is a God, and if he is anything like the God who is revealed to us in the Scriptures, then it would be extremely presumptuous, foolish, and (by all accounts) dangerous for us to crowdsource our own ethical code.

The law is an expression of the Lawgiver's heart and character. We must think about that before we say, "I don't care for laws," or before we bristle at the thought of do's and don'ts. The commandments not only show us what God wants; they show us what God is like. They say something about his honor, his worth, and his majesty. They tell us what matters to God. We can't disdain the law without disrespecting the Lawgiver.

Reason 3: Who God Is to Us

The God of the Ten Commandments is revealed not just as the Lord, but as the "Lord *your* God" (Ex. 20:2). We are his treasured possession (Ex. 19:5; 1 Pet. 2:9). This God of absolute power is not a capricious tyrant, not some cranky deity who wields raw and unbridled authority without any regard for his creatures. He is a personal God, and in Christ he always is for us (Rom. 8:31). It would be frightening to the point of death if God thundered from the heavens, "I am the Lord!" But the divine self-disclosure doesn't stop there. He goes on to add, ". . . your God." He is on our side. He is our Father. He gives us commands for our good.

Reason 4: Where We Are

The biblical definition of freedom is not "doing whatever you want." Freedom is enjoying the benefits of doing what we should. We too often think of the Ten Commandments as constraining us—as if God's ways will keep us in servitude and from realizing our dreams and reaching our potential. We forget that God means to give us abundant life (John 10:10) and true freedom (John 8:32). His laws, 1 John 5:3 tells us, are not burdensome.

You think it's burdensome to have Ten Commandments? Do you know how many laws there are in the United States? It's a trick question, because no one knows! There are twenty thousand laws on the books regulating gun ownership alone. In 2010 an estimated forty thousand new laws were added at various levels throughout the country. The United States Code, which is just one accounting of federal laws and does not include regulatory statutes, has more than fifty volumes. In 2008 a House committee asked the Congressional Research Service to calculate the number of criminal offenses in federal law. They responded, five years later, that they lacked the manpower and resources to answer such a question.[5]

God is not trying to crush us with red tape and regulations. The Ten Commandments are not prison bars, but traffic laws. Maybe there are some anarchists out there who think, "The world would be a better place without any traffic laws." A few of us drive as if that were so! But even if you get impatient when you're at a red light, try to zoom through the yellow, and turn left on a very stale pink—overall, aren't you glad that there is some semblance of law and order? People stop and go. People slow down when driving by schools. They stop for school buses. You wouldn't be able to drive your car to the grocery store without laws. When you drive on a switchback on a mountain pass, do you curse the guardrails that keep you from plunging to an untimely death? No, someone put them there at great expense, and for our good, that we may travel about freely and safely.

The Ten Commandments are not instructions on how to get out of Egypt. They are rules for a free people to stay free.

Reason 5: What He Has Done

Note once again that the law comes after gospel—after the good news of deliverance. God did not come to the people as slaves and say, "I have Ten Commandments. I want you to get these right. I'm going to come back in five years, and if you've gotten your life cleaned up, I'll set you free from Egypt." That's how some people view Christianity: God has rules, and if I follow the rules, God will love me and save me. That's not what happened in the story of the exodus. The Israelites were an oppressed people, and God said, "I hear your cry. I will save you because I love you. And when you are saved, free, and forgiven, I'm going to give you a new way to live."

We need to hear it again: salvation is not the *reward* for obedience; salvation is the *reason* for obedience. Jesus does not say, "If you obey my commandments, I will love you." Instead, he first washes the feet of the disciples and then says, "If you love me, you will keep my commandments" (John 14:15). All of our doing is only because of what he has first done for us.

1

God and God Alone

You shall have no other gods before me.

Exodus 20:3

If our faith is to be genuine Christian faith, it must be more than faith in faith. The most important aspect of our faith is not how hard we believe, but in whom we believe. There is certainly a subjective element to faith—since we do want to be sincere and single-minded in our devotion—but to have a sincerely misguided belief in the wrong thing or in the wrong person is not saving faith at all. It's possible to be full of sincere worship and worship the wrong God. That's the reason for the first commandment.

The God of the Bible is not simply interested in being recognized as a strong and mighty deity. That would not have been a controversial claim in the ancient world. Lots of peoples had lots of impressive gods and goddesses. What *was* controversial, and what set the Israelites apart from the other nations, was that their

God demanded to be worshiped *alone,* as the *only* God, to the *ex-clusion* of all others.

There's a reason that the first commandment is the first commandment. It's not that this one is better than all the others, but it is foundational for all the others. Because there is only one God, who is God over all and has divine rights over all, we can have the subsequent nine commandments—an objective moral code that isn't just true for some people, in some places, depending upon their circumstances, but is true for all people everywhere.

Can a truly authoritative moral law exist without the existence of a divine lawgiver? The obvious answer, according to the Bible, is that it cannot. If our moral obligations are to have any force or binding obligation behind them, they must rest on something more than majority opinion, our own internal sense of right and wrong, or (heaven forbid) an Internet poll. Remember what the ten noncommandments had for the ninth commandment: "There is no one right way to live." That one commandment eliminates the force of the other nine. The noncommandment commandments, because they have no place for God, end up having all the force of internally contradictory suggestions.

What Christianity Hath Wrought

It may appear to many in the secular West that God is irrelevant in determining right from wrong. But it only appears that way because Christianity has been at the center of Western culture for so long. People do not realize where their ethical instincts come from. Recently there was a fascinating article by the popular and well-respected British historian Tom Holland. I don't know if Holland is claiming to be a Christian in the article, but he is certainly describing how he rediscovered that his morality is owing to Christianity.[1]

Holland tells his story of growing up in the church. From an early age, he started to have doubts about what he was learning in his Sunday school class, and he began to question everything about his Christian environment. Later, as he became a scholar of ancient antiquity, a writer, and a historian, he became enamored with the Greco-Roman world, in part as a foil to the benighted Christian age that would follow.

> By the time I came to read Edward Gibbon and the other great writers of the Enlightenment, I was more than ready to accept their interpretation of history: that the triumph of Christianity had ushered in an "age of superstition and credulity," and that modernity was founded on the dusting down of long-forgotten classical values.[2]

In short, Holland came to believe that the values worth emulating came from the Greeks and the Romans. He concluded that Christianity introduced a backwards sort of spirituality and gullibility. But listen to what Holland says next:

> The longer I spent immersed in the study of classical antiquity, the more alien and unsettling I came to find it. The values of Leonidas [a leader of the Spartans], whose people had practised a peculiarly murderous form of eugenics, and trained their young to kill uppity Untermenschen by night, were nothing that I recognised as my own; nor were those of Caesar, who was reported to have killed a million Gauls and enslaved a million more. It was not just the extremes of callousness that I came to find shocking, but the lack of a sense that the poor or the weak might have any intrinsic value. As such, the founding conviction of the Enlightenment—that it owed nothing to the faith into which most of its greatest figures had been born—increasingly came to seem to me unsustainable.[3]

In other words, the more he studied the history of antiquity, the more Holland wondered if his sense of morality—and that of his friends—really came from Christianity.

> Familiarity with the biblical narrative of the Crucifixion has dulled our sense of just how completely novel a deity Christ was. In the ancient world, it was the role of gods who laid claim to ruling the universe to uphold its order by inflicting punishment—not to suffer it themselves. Today, even as belief in God fades across the West, the countries that were once collectively known as Christendom continue to bear the stamp of the two-millennia-old revolution that Christianity represents. It is the principal reason why, by and large, most of us who live in post-Christian societies still take for granted that it is nobler to suffer than to inflict suffering. It is why we generally assume that every human life is of equal value. In my morals and ethics, I have learned to accept that I am not Greek or Roman at all, but thoroughly and proudly Christian.[4]

I don't know what Holland thinks of the Ten Commandments, but he's done an excellent job summarizing the influence of Christian principles and the need for an ethical code outside ourselves. We have a moral code because we have a moral Lawgiver. The only reason that the Ten Commandments can have any sort of binding obligation upon or authority over us is that there is a God who created us, made us, loves us, and has rights over us. The first commandment not only gives us our first obligation as human beings; it lays the groundwork for every other moral obligation.

———

So how do we keep the first commandment? It's helpful to see why the commandment matters and how it has shaped our ethical reasoning, but the point of the commandment is that we do what it commands. Let me suggest, then, three ways we keep the first commandment: worship God exclusively, shun all idolatry, and turn to Christ uniquely.

Worship God Exclusively

The first commandment is predicated on what the Lord did for the Israelites in Egypt. He saved them. He rescued them. He delivered them. He has a claim over them. When God says, "I am the LORD your God, who brought you out of the land of Egypt" (Ex. 20:2), he is reminding them of the staff, the plagues, and the Red Sea. He's saying to them, "Why would you trust any other so-called god? Why would you trust yourself? You didn't escape Egypt by your own ingenuity or because of Pharaoh's great kindness. I put you on eagles' wings. I defeated mighty Egypt. You can trust me."

We must not misunderstand the phrase "no other gods before me." The first commandment is not suggesting that there are, in fact, other gods. There's a view called *henotheism,* which says there are many gods, but you must give your god first place. That's not what the first commandment is about. The Mosaic covenant clearly presumes *monotheism.* No other gods should be worshiped because in reality there are no gods but Yahweh. This is the point Paul makes centuries later when he says:

> Therefore, as to the eating of food offered to idols, we know that "an idol has no real existence," and that "there is no God but one." For although there may be so-called gods in heaven or on earth—as indeed there are many "gods" and many "lords"—yet for us there is one God, the Father, from whom are all things and for whom we exist, and one Lord, Jesus Christ, through whom are all things and through whom we exist. (1 Cor. 8:4–6)

The gods of this world are only so-called gods. They have no ontological existence. There is only one supreme being in the universe, and he demands to be worshiped alone.

Already in the first verse of the Bible we see that Israel's God is unique among the pantheon of (supposed) deities: "In the beginning, God created the heavens and the earth" (Gen. 1:1). That sounds right to us, but it would have been unusual in the ancient Near East. The ancients had lots of stories about how the universe came into being, but they always involved two gods fighting, or a god and a goddess procreating, or one god slaying another god and forming the earth out of its carcass. By contrast, Genesis comes along and says, "In the beginning, there was only one God, the real God, and he created all things." This would have been a shocking way to begin a religious text. "Monotheism," as John Dickson puts it, "is not just the Bible's first commandment, it is its first thought."[5]

Syncretism was a perennial problem in Israel. God's people were constantly tempted to make their faith a both/and religion, when God insisted on worship as an either/or proposition: "*Either* you worship me alone, *or* you don't worship me at all." When the covenant was renewed at Shechem, Joshua exhorted the people, "Put away the gods that your fathers served beyond the River and in Egypt, and serve the LORD" (Josh. 24:14). On Mount Carmel, Elijah said much the same: "If the LORD is God, follow him; but if Baal, then follow him" (1 Kings 18:21). Years later, Jesus would remind his followers that "no one can serve two masters, for either he will hate the one and love the other, or he will be devoted to the one and despise the other" (Matt. 6:24).

The fault with God's people has always been that little *and*. The Lord is fine, but we want the Lord *and* Baal, the Lord *and* Asherah, the Lord *and* money, the Lord *and* social respectability. We're quite happy to have God in our lives, just so long as he fills only a part of our lives. We all want a Trivial Pursuit God, a manageable deity to round out our lives and fill in one piece of the pie. But he has no interest in being one important person among many. God cannot be worshiped rightly if he is worshiped alongside any other.

The other nine commandments speak of acts you should or shouldn't do, but the first commandment mandates a certain kind of relationship. It tells us how we are to relate to God as the only God. When Exodus 20:3 says, "No other gods before me," it could mean "none other but me," or it could mean "no other gods before my face." Calvin understood the commandment in the latter sense. He said that the sin here is "like a shameless woman who brings in an adulterer before her husband's very eyes, only to vex his mind the more."[6]

Regardless of how we interpret "before me," marriage is a good analogy for the first commandment. You cannot have a both/and relationship with your spouse—at least, not for very long. Suppose a husband came home and said, "Honey, it's good to see you! I want to introduce someone who's very special to me. Don't get me wrong—you're also very special to me. But I've met someone else. She's lovely, and I'm going to spend some time with her, but also a lot of time with you! I just want to let you know that some nights, I'm going to be with her instead. I think you two will get along just fine. You'll be great friends. You both mean so much to me."

What should a wife say in this situation? "That's great, dear, I'm honored that I can still be a part of your life." Hardly! The wife would say, "It's me or her! Make up your mind." And if the wife were to say that with a great deal of passion, would anyone think she was being cruel, proud, unfair, or intolerant? No, we would say that she's being just the sort of wife she ought to be. She has every right to be jealous. We'd be concerned if she wasn't angry. Some relationships are meant to be either/or, not both/and. Marriage is a relationship that demands forsaking all others.

And so it is with God. Love is at the very heart of the first commandment. If we truly love God, we will love no one else and nothing else like we love God. That's why the Shema was so foundational for the Israelites: "Hear, O Israel: The LORD our God, the LORD is one. You shall love the LORD your God with all your heart and with all your soul and with all your might" (Deut. 6:4–5). Love suggests affection, but it is also a decision. The Shema called God's people to choose the Lord as God, and him alone. We choose God because he first chose us. And now, forsaking all others, we commit ourselves to him unreservedly. There can be no *and* in our relationship with God. We love and worship him above all others because he alone is God.

Shun All Idolatry

The Heidelberg Catechism defines idolatry as "having or inventing something in which one trusts in place of or alongside of the only true God, who has revealed himself in his Word."[7] Though most Westerners aren't tempted to bow down before trees and statues, we'd be foolish to think that we don't have the same propensity for idolatry that they had in ancient Israel. While we may know on an intellectual level that we can make food or family or football into an idol, we don't often stop to think about the perennial attraction of idolatry. The same forces at work in the ancient world that made idolatry attractive are still with us today, pulling us and prodding us to trust something or someone else alongside the only true God.

One of the best summaries of the attraction of idolatry comes from the Old Testament scholar Doug Stuart. In his Exodus commentary, he lists nine reasons the Israelites were so drawn to idolatry:[8]

1. *It was guaranteed.* If they did the right incantation, it worked. If they said the right words, God showed up. Who wouldn't want a religion with guaranteed results?

2. *It was selfish.* In the ancient world, the gods (though they were powerful) needed the humans for one very important thing: food. It was understood that people needed to bring sacrifices because the gods were hungry. The people needed the gods for favors; the gods needed the people if they were to eat. It was a tit-for-tat relationship. You scratch their backs; they'll scratch yours.

3. *It was easy.* Sure, one had to bring offerings and oblations, but there was little in the way of ethical standards or personal sacrifice. A good Canaanite didn't need an elaborate moral code or a rigorous pursuit of personal holiness. He just had to show up and present a drink or a dead animal. That's what Israel fell into, time and time again: "It doesn't really matter what I do. I just have to show up and go through the religious rituals."

4. *It was convenient.* Ancient worship worked on a franchise model. There were many places one could go to take care of his religious obligations. Again, this was part of the allure of idolatry for the Israelites. Why not build a few high places? Why not make worship a little more convenient? But Yahweh has prescribed ritual worship in one place: at the tabernacle, and later in the temple.

5. *It was normal.* Everyone else—though their gods had different names and did different things—did religion the same way. The Israelites were unique among the people of the ancient Near East. God's people didn't just have a few special rules; their conception of the divine and how to worship him was fundamentally different. It's hard to be a religious minority.

6. *It was logical.* It made sense that there were many gods and goddesses, each one specializing in an area of blessing

and an area of the cosmos. One god brought the wind, another one summoned the rain, and another helped the animals breed. Religion in the ancient world seemed to make sense of the world around them.

7. *It was pleasing to the senses*. There was always plenty to see. There was even an aesthetic element to ancient worship, with beauty and craftsmanship on obvious display. Idolatry was right in front of them. Seeing was believing.

8. *It was indulgent*. Meat was a relative rarity in the ancient world. Most people didn't have extra animals to slaughter, so they tended to eat meat only as a part of ritual worship. They would sacrifice an animal and present a drink offering, and then feast together with their family or clan. Idolatry was an occasion for eating the best food and drinking the best wine.

9. *It was erotic*. Many ancients believed that in order to get blessings from the gods, they needed them to mate together in the heavens. If Baal and Asherah hooked up, then their procreation in the heavens would yield fruitful harvests and offspring on earth. But how could they get the divine romance started? The answer was to have sex themselves. That's why we find cult prostitutes throughout the Old Testament. The ancients believed that if they had sex as a part of religious ritual, then the gods and goddesses would have sex too.

It's not hard to see why idolatry was so attractive and why Israel was constantly tempted to adopt the same practices. The religion of the world was guaranteed, selfish, easy, convenient, normal, logical, pleasing, indulgent, and erotic. It was a religious system made by men, for men.

When we understand the nature of ancient idolatry, it's easy to see how we are tempted by the same things. We are just as interested as they were in worship that is entertaining, satisfying, and practical. Our idols look different, but it's those same idols of sex and ease and convenience that we desire thousands of years later.

Turn to Christ Uniquely

As we'll see throughout these studies, this first commandment (like the others) is transformed by the coming of Christ. By "transformed" I don't mean that God says, "These commandments don't apply to you anymore." But the way they apply—and the way we obey them—does change.

Perhaps "transposed" is even a better word than "transformed." When a piece of music is transposed, the melody stays the same, but it's played in a different octave or a different key. That's sort of how the Ten Commandments change from the Old Testament to the New. It's the same score, different key. These commandments are still commandments for the church, but they have all been transposed by the coming of Christ.

We can think of this first commandment, in relationship to Christ, as a tale of two mountains. God came down on Mount Sinai, saying, "Worship me alone." Then, millennia later, he came down on the Mount of Transfiguration and said, "This is my beloved Son . . . ; listen to him" (Matt. 17:5). It's amazing that the God who said, "Worship me, and listen to my rules," now tells us to listen to his Son.

On the other side of the incarnation, the first commandment means giving to Christ the worship he deserves. He is the "one mediator between God and men" (1 Tim. 2:5). He is "the radiance of the glory of God and the exact imprint of his nature" (Heb. 1:3). He is the one before whom everyone will bow in worship

(Phil. 2:10–11). As Jesus himself says, "If you had known me, you would have known my Father also. From now on you do know him and have seen him" (John 14:7). In other words, Jesus has the audacity to say, "If you know me, you know God. If you follow me, love me, and worship me, you worship God. When you see me, you have seen God in the flesh."

The implication from all this is that if you don't know God in Christ, then you don't really know God. The first commandment can no longer be properly obeyed unless we worship the one who alone shows us the one true God. It isn't enough to use the word *God* or to belong to a monotheistic religion. We are not worshiping the one true God unless we are worshiping the God and Father of our Lord Jesus Christ. The coming of Christ has changed everything.

Four Closing Questions

In his commentary on the first commandment, Calvin argues that we owe God four things: adoration, trust, invocation, and thanksgiving.[9] Each of these can be applied to Christ as we seek to obey the first commandment. In adoration, we worship Christ. In trust, we treasure Christ. In invocation, we look to Christ. In thanksgiving, we find grace in Christ. That's how we obey the first commandment as New Testament Christians.

We can use these same four points to ask four diagnostic questions. These will help us determine not just what we *say* we believe but the nature of the *real* functional deity in our lives.

1. Whom do you praise (adoration)? You may compliment your children, spouse, and friends, but who receives your highest praise?

2. Whom do you count on (trust)? Sure, God works through means, such as doctors, insurance companies, and pre-

scription medicine, but when you really are in need, who do you know will always come through?

3. Whom do you call for (invocation)? Where do you look for answers? Where do you turn for purpose and joy? Is it food, work, TV, your phone, or the God of the universe?

4. Whom do you thank? Where do your good days come from? Who made the trees and the stars and that cooing little baby?

Questions like these help to reveal the real gods in our lives. For the one we praise, the one we count on, the one we call for, and the one we thank is the one we worship. Only in Christ can we find satisfying and saving answers to all those questions. Only in him can we truly obey the first commandment. He alone is worthy, willing, and mighty to save.

2

The Way of Worship

You shall not make for yourself a carved image, or any likeness of anything that is in heaven above, or that is in the earth beneath, or that is in the water under the earth. You shall not bow down to them or serve them, for I the LORD your God am a jealous God, visiting the iniquity of the fathers on the children to the third and the fourth generation of those who hate me, but showing steadfast love to thousands of those who love me and keep my commandments.

Exodus 20:4–6

There's a story in the New Testament where Paul visits the great city of Athens. Like Oxford or Cambridge or Boston, Athens was a famous intellectual city, renowned for its history, its learning, and its contribution to culture. Athens was said to be the glory of Greece.

And yet have you ever noticed Paul's reaction when residing in this world-class city? Was Paul impressed with its intellect? Did he fall in love with its architecture? Was he amazed by their food?

Acts records that "his spirit was provoked within him as he saw that the city was full of idols" (17:16). Later he says to Athenians, in effect, "Look, I can see you are very religious. You have temples and rituals and statues all over the place. You are really into worship. But I'm telling you: you're going about it in the wrong way" (see Acts 17:22–23). That's why Paul was provoked in his spirit. He could see that no matter how spiritual or how smart or how sincere they may have been, they were worshiping God in a way that did not please him.

If the first commandment is against worshiping the wrong God, the second commandment is against worshiping God in the wrong way. The people in Athens were guilty of both. They were ignorant of the God who raised Jesus from the dead, *and* their approach to religion was not what the true God had prescribed.

Self-Willed Worship

Most generally, the second commandment forbids self-willed worship—worshiping God as we choose rather than as he demands. In particular, the second commandment makes two prohibitions:

1. We are not to make images to represent God in any form.
2. We are not to worship images of any kind.

The second commandment does not intend to outlaw art or painting or aesthetic considerations. The tabernacle displayed angels and palm trees, the ark will have cherubim, and God himself gave the Spirit to Bezalel and Oholiab that they might be skilled artists and craftsmen. God is not against beauty. What he prohibits is infusing any object with spiritual efficacy, as if man-made artifacts can bring us closer to God, represent God, or establish communion with God.

The Old Testament is full of examples of God's people using man-made artifacts for self-willed worship. The golden calf is the most famous example. Remember, Aaron proclaimed a feast to *Yahweh*, and the people declared that *these* were the gods who brought them up out of Egypt (Ex. 32:4–5). The Israelites weren't worshiping Baal. They were trying to worship the Lord their God, but they were doing it in the wrong way. They were violating the second commandment.

At other times, the Israelites treated their religious symbols as though they had real religious powers. This too was a violation of the second commandment, turning the ark into some kind of talisman (1 Sam. 4:1–11) or treating the temple like a good luck charm (Jer. 7:1–15). We can do the same with church buildings or pulpits or the cross around our neck.

Like most of the Decalogue, the second commandment is not hard to understand. The *what* is fairly straightforward. The *why* and *how* take some more explanation. To that end, I want to give five reasons for the prohibitions in the second commandment and then five ways to apply the second commandment in our lives. But before we get to the command itself, we need to look at one other aspect of the commandment.

Sins and Souls

What are we to make of the threat in verse 5 to visit the iniquity of the fathers on their children? This warning is repeated elsewhere in the Old Testament (Ex. 34:6–7; Num. 14:18; Jer. 32:18). But what does it mean?

It's not a reference to generational curses, hexes, or demonic oppression. Nor does it mean that a righteous child will be punished unfairly for the sins of his wicked father. That's a common misunderstanding from verse 5, so common, it seems, that Ezekiel 18 means to correct it. In Ezekiel 18:20 we read, "The soul who sins shall die. The son shall not suffer for the iniquity of the father, nor the father suffer for the iniquity of the son." God does not say to a righteous child, "Tough break, kid, your dad was wicked, so I'm going to really let you have it." The book of Ezekiel will not let us take that view of the second commandment.

So what *does* the warning mean? This warning is about God's judgment on those who walk in the wicked ways of their parents and grandparents and great-grandparents. Look at verse 5 carefully. God says he will visit "the iniquity of the fathers to the third and the fourth generation of those who *hate* me." The children share in their father's punishment because they share in their father's sins. Ezekiel teaches that if you turn away from your father's sin, you will not face your father's punishment. But Exodus says, if you keep on sinning as your father did, you will not escape your father's punishment. You can't say, "I'm only doing what my parents taught me." You can't excuse your disobedience by pointing to your upbringing or culture or personal history. God will punish the next generation if they continue in the sins they learned from the previous generation. That's the point of the warning.

And don't forget there is a promise alongside the threat. God will show mercy to thousands (or to a thousand generations) of those who love him. This is not a precise math formula, as if Moses's obedience meant that his children twenty thousand years later, roughly one thousand generations, would automatically be holy. The promise of steadfast love is for those who "keep my commandments," just like the threat of punishment is for "those who hate me."

No One Like Him

As we turn back to the commandment itself, let me start by suggesting five reasons God forbids images and anything else to represent him in worship.

First, *God is free.* Once you have something to represent God or worship as if it were God, you undermine God's freedom. We start to think we can bring God with us by carrying around a statue. Or we think we can manage God with the right rituals. Or we think he'll be our benefactor if we simply pray in a certain direction or make an offering before a graven image. Anytime we make something in order to see God, or see something that stands in for God, we are undermining his freedom. God is Spirit, and he doesn't have a body (John 4:24). It is not for us to make the invisible God visible.

Second, *God is jealous.* No image will capture God's glory. Every man-made representation of the Divine will be so far less than God as to incite his jealousy. Think about it: the more chaste and pure a husband, the more his jealousy is aroused by an adulterous wife. God is supremely pure, and he cannot bear to share his glory with another, even if the other is a sincere attempt to represent (and not replace) the one true God. God is a being unto himself. In fact, he *is* being. His glory cannot be captured in a picture or an image or a form. That's why even in Revelation when we have a vision of the One on the throne, he is "shown" to us in visual metaphors: lightning, rainbow, colors, sea, fire, lamps, thrones, etc.

The world of the ancient Near East divinized everything. The Israelites divinized nothing—not Father Time or Mother Earth or the sun or the moon or the stars. The separation between God and his creation is one of the defining characteristics of biblical Christianity. Any human attempt to bridge that chasm is not only an attempt at the impossible but an affront to the unparalleled majesty of God.

Third, *believing sight comes by sound.* In the Bible, especially on this side of heaven, we see by hearing. As Deuteronomy later made clear, the Sinai experience was a paradigm for God's self-revelation. When the Lord appeared to the people on the mountain out of the midst of fire, Moses reminded them, "You heard the sound of words, but saw no form; there was only a voice" (Deut. 4:12). And because they saw no form, the Israelites were commanded not to corrupt themselves by making visible images (4:15ff.).

We make no apology for being Word-centered and words-centered. Faith comes by hearing (Rom. 10:17). That's how God designed it because that's how he has chosen to reveal himself. Christian worship is meant to be wordy and not a breathtaking visual display. If God wanted us to see him in worship, he would have presented himself differently in the Sinai theophany. The way God "showed up" to give the Ten Commandments says something about how we are to keep the Ten Commandments.

Fourth, *God provides his own mediators*. At their best, God's people have employed images and icons not because they thought God could be housed in a marble bust, but in order to provide more intimate access to God. If God is in heaven, it makes sense that we would want a little portal for him here on earth. But God's people should know better. The saints in the Old Testament did not need to fashion an intermediary for themselves; God had already promised mediators through the prophets, priests, and kings. God had his own way to draw near to his people, culminating in a final Mediator who would embrace all three offices at once and pitch his tent among us (John 1:14).

Fifth, *we don't need to create images of God because he has already created them*. The implications of Genesis 1:26–27 are staggering. *We* are the divinely chosen statues meant to show what God is like, created in his image and after his likeness. Idolatry diminishes God *and* diminishes us. In Ezekiel 18:11–13, right in the middle of a host of horizontal, neighborly sins, is the mention of idolatry. Why? Because mistreating other people and worshiping idols have the same root: a violation of the divine image. In one case, we are looking for God's image where it doesn't exist (idolatry), and in the other case we are ignoring God's image where it does exist (sins against our neighbors). We are God's statues in the world, marking out the planet as his and his alone. He does not need our help in making more images; he asks for our witness.

Keeping the Commandment Today

If that's *why* we keep the second commandment, we still have to consider *how* we keep the second commandment. Following are five ways.

First, *guard against images of God both external and imagined.* As we've just seen, the second commandment is about more than obvious Baal worship. It's about the freedom and jealousy of our invisible God. We must avoid infusing any created things with divine immanence and spiritual efficacy. This doesn't mean we have to trash all our nativity sets and angel ornaments and artwork on the wall. But it does mean that using pictures or icons to focus us in prayer, let alone kissing or kneeling before an image or statue, is misplaced.

And the old distinction between worship (bad) and veneration (good) will not do. Imagine the Israelites saying that the golden calf was not for worship but just an object for veneration. God would not have been impressed with the tortured logic. As the Reformers used to say, look at what they do, not at what they say. If we bow to the image, relic, or icon, or focus on it, or think we need it to be closer to God, it's a violation of the second commandment.

We must also guard against mental images of God. I'm not talking about the picture of a shepherd popping into your head when you read that Christ is the Good Shepherd. I'm talking about some strands of evangelical piety where we are told to picture God running to you. Or we are instructed to close our eyes and imagine

God's arms around us. To be sure, we may want to *compare* God's love to a warm embrace or imagine God is *like* a father running to greet his prodigal son, but we ought not make images of the invisible God, even if they are only in our imagination. As the Westminster Larger Catechism puts it, the second commandment forbids "the making any representation of God, or all or any of the three persons, either inwardly in our mind, or outwardly in any kind of image or likeness of any creature whatsoever."[1]

Second, *don't contribute to the idolatry of others*. It's worth noting that the first commandment, in saying "You shall not have," speaks of possession, while the second commandment, in saying "You shall not make," speaks of manufacturing. True, the "make" is followed by "for yourself," so personal idolatry is in view. But it's also fair to see a prohibition against the manufacturing of idols that others might use. Where idolatry looks less overt than golden totems, we would do well to consider whether we are producing, selling, advertising, or pushing goods and services that lead people away from true worship of the true and living God.

Third, *consider the wisdom of the regulative principle*. Even though I grew up in a Reformed church, until seminary I was one of the multitude of Christians who had never heard of the regulative principle. It's not something I've always been passionate about. But over the years I've come to appreciate the regulative principle more and more. Simply put, the regulative principle states that "the acceptable way of worshiping the true God is instituted by himself and so limited by his own revealed will."[2] In other words, corporate worship should be comprised of those elements we can show to be appropriate from the Bible. The regulative principle says, "Let's worship God as he wants to be worshiped." Or as the Heidelberg Catechism puts it, God's will for us in the second commandment is "that we in no way make any image of God nor worship him in any other way than he has commanded in his Word."[3]

At its worst, the regulative principle leads to constant friction and suspicion between believers. But at the heart of the principle is freedom, not restriction—freedom from cultural captivity, freedom from weekly novelties, and freedom from man-made ideas and preferences. The regulative principle says we don't have to guess about what pleases God in worship. We can obey the second commandment by worshiping God as he commands us in his Word.

Fourth, *let's remedy the ignorance of God's people by giving them what they need, not necessarily what they want.* During the Reformation, as a more Word-centered (and words-centered) approach to worship took hold across Europe, some religious leaders argued in favor of images because they were considered the books of the laity. They argued, in effect, "Look, people can't read. They don't understand complicated doctrine. But they can learn about the Christian faith from icons and statues and stained-glass windows." The Reformers said, in turn, "Well, then, we must teach the people." When faced with the choice between adorning the spectacle and educating the people, they firmly sided with the latter.

The circumstances look different in our day, but the principles are the same. Many Christian leaders seek to build services around people's felt needs. Or they spare no expense in putting on an elaborate production Sunday after Sunday. While the motivations may be pure (or not), God's way is to build up his people by edifying teaching, not by entertaining theater. We don't want to be snobbish, or elitist, or assume that people know more than they do. But neither do we want to always "meet people where they are at." God's design for worship has always been countercultural. What we win them with is what we win them to. Let us opt for the slow, patient approach of teaching the Bible bit by bit. After all, in the beginning was the Word (John 1:1), not a play, a picture, or a production.

Fifth, *look to Christ as the fulfillment of the second commandment*. There is considerable disagreement among thoughtful Christians about how the incarnation may change our keeping of the second commandment. Some argue that Jesus represents the "breaking" of the second commandment. He made the invisible God visible. Thereafter, we are not wrong to draw pictures of Jesus or show pictures to our children. While I sympathize with the argument and agree that there is a difference between an obviously artistic or childlike drawing of Jesus and an image we create to look like him or to help focus our hearts in worship, I still think we honor the commandment best by keeping the invisible God invisible.

The truth is we don't know what Jesus looked like, and the Bible makes no effort to give us a physical description. And yet how many of us in the West can't help but think of Jesus as a long-haired, high-cheek-boned, Teutonic man with a far-off gaze, simply because we've seen so many pictures and portraits and videos where he looks just like this?

Regardless of our convictions about pictures of Jesus, we ought to recognize that Christ has uniquely fulfilled the second commandment. He showed forth the Father to his disciples (John 14:9). To look upon Christ was to look upon the face of him who could not be seen on Sinai. Jesus did the seemingly impossible. He allowed humans to see the God who cannot be seen. That's the mystery and majesty of the incarnation. We don't need pictures. We don't need statues. We don't need icons. We have the icon: Christ is the image (*eikon*) of the invisible God (Col. 1:15).

3

What's in a Name?

You shall not take the name of the LORD your God in vain,
for the LORD will not hold him guiltless who takes his name
in vain.

Exodus 20:7

> 'Tis but thy name that is my enemy:
> Thou art thyself, though not a Montague.
> What's Montague? It is nor hand nor foot,
> Nor arm nor face, nor any other part
> Belonging to a man. O, be some other name!
> What's in a name? That which we call a rose
> By any other word would smell as sweet;
> So Romeo would, were he not Romeo call'd,
> Retain that dear perfection which he owes
> Without that title. Romeo, doff thy name,
> And for that name which is no part of thee
> Take all myself.

These lines, of course, come from Shakespeare's famous play
Romeo and Juliet.[1] The story is about two star-crossed lov-
ers whose romance is forbidden because they come from rival

families. He's a Montague; she's a Capulet. If only they were called by something else, they could be free to love and to live together.

But as Romeo and Juliet found out, names are not so easily discarded. "What's in a name?" More than we might think. While it's true that a rose by any other name would smell as sweet, would roses be as popular if they were called "corpse flower" or "lung wart"?

Parents understand that one of the most important things they do for their children is the first thing they do for their children: give them a name. Most of us take this responsibility very seriously. We consult genealogies and family histories. We get one of those thick books of baby names. We look online at the most popular names from the last year. We scour the Bible for obscure names no one has ever heard of. We look at every possible angle through which someone might be able to make fun of our child's name or initials. Names matter to us—big time.

My wife and I have a lot of kids, so it can be tricky to choose good names for the younger ones. We have a son named Jacob, so Esau is pretty much out of the question. We've always liked the name Joseph but opted for Benjamin instead (for our sixth child), because we realized that we already had a Mary—and Mary and Joseph would be a bit much, even for a pastor's family. We also considered the name Peter, a family name on my side, but we also have a Paul—and you can't name your kids Peter, Paul, and Mary. These are the sort of things you have to think about as a parent. Names matter—to us and to our kids.

And, as it turns out, names also matter to God.

A Commandment Not to Be Taken in Vain

The first commandment prohibited the worship of false gods. We can understand why that's a big deal. After all, you can't go around worshiping the wrong god. And the second commandment prohibited worshiping God in the wrong way. That makes sense too. An invisible God has the right to determine how he is to be made visible (or not). The first two commandments seem pretty foundational.

If we're honest, though, when we come to the third commandment, we feel like we can let our guard down just a little. "Watch what you say. Don't swear. Be careful with your OMGs." Got it. The third commandment feels less like a bedrock principle and more like a good reminder.

But if we think violating the third commandment is a light offense, we are quite mistaken. In Leviticus 24:16 we read, "Whoever blasphemes the name of the LORD shall surely be put to death. All the congregation shall stone him. The sojourner as well as the native, when he blasphemes the Name, shall be put to death." Granted, this is a civil law for the nation of Israel. The parallel for us would be church discipline, not public execution (1 Cor. 5:9–13). But the Levitical instruction clearly shows us the severity of the sin. Even the sojourner was liable to punishment. Whether you were visiting Israel or native born, it was to be understood that the name of the Lord was holy and not to be blasphemed under any circumstance.

The *What*

So what exactly is forbidden by the third commandment? The word *vain* (as it's rendered in the ESV) can mean "empty," "nothing," "worthless," or "to no good purpose." We are forbidden, therefore, from taking the name of God (or *taking up* the name or *bearing* the name, as the phrase could be translated) in a manner that is wicked, worthless, or for wrong purposes. This doesn't mean that we have to avoid the divine name altogether. The name YHWH (or Yahweh)—"the LORD," in most translations—appears some seven thousand times in the Old Testament. We don't need to be superstitious about saying his name. But we must not misuse it.

The Old Testament identifies several ways in which the third commandment can be violated. Most obvious is to blaspheme or curse the name of God, which we saw already in Leviticus 24:16. But there's more to the commandment than that.

The third commandment also forbids empty or false oaths: "You shall not swear by my name falsely, and so profane the name of your God: I am the LORD" (Lev. 19:12; cf. Hos. 10:4a). When you make a declaration, swearing by God's name, it must not be a false promise or one you do not intend to keep.

The third commandment also prohibits false visions and false claims to speak on God's behalf, for such prophets "prophesy lies in my name" (Jer. 23:25).

Strangely enough, sacrificing one's children to the false god Molech was considered a violation of the third commandment because it profaned the name of God (Lev. 18:21). The Israelites were to stone the man who sacrificed his children in this way. Failure to do so would allow for uncleanness to permeate the camp, thereby besmirching the name of the Lord, who dwelt in the midst of his people.

Similarly, to unlawfully touch the holy things was considered a violation of the third commandment. We read in Leviticus 22: "Speak to Aaron and his sons so that they abstain from the holy things of the people of Israel, which they dedicate to me, so that they do not profane my holy name: I am the LORD" (v. 2). Likewise, the priests who cut corners in Malachi's day were devaluing the name of God by their polluted offerings and cynical hearts (Mal. 1:10–14).

The *Why*

We've already seen that breaking the third commandment is considered a terribly serious sin, but why? There are only ten commandments, after all. Only ten words to summarize everything God wants from us by way of obedience. How did "watch your mouth" make the top ten? What's the big deal about God's name?

Think about Exodus 3 where God speaks to Moses from the burning bush. Moses asks God, "If I come to the people of Israel and say to them, 'The God of your fathers has sent me to you,' and they ask me, 'What is his name?' what shall I say to them?" God replies with those famous words: "I AM WHO I AM. . . . Say this to the people of Israel: 'I AM has sent me to you'" (Ex. 3:13–14). God names himself as the sovereign, self-existent one. In fact, the covenant name YHWH is probably connected to the Hebrew verb "to be." God is that he is. That is his name.

We see the same thing in Exodus 33. Moses asks God to *show* him his glory. And in reply, God *speaks* to him his name: "I will make all my goodness pass before you and will proclaim before you my name 'The LORD'" (v. 19a). The way to see God's glory is to hear his name. To know the name YHWH, the merciful and gracious one, is not to merely know something about God; it is to know God himself (Ex. 34:6–8). God shows himself by speaking his name.

Our name is not tangential to our being. It marks us and identifies us. Over time, as people get to know us, our name embodies who we are. Think of someone whom you love deeply—your child, grandchild, parent, friend, or spouse. The name of that person represents more than markings on a page. When someone says the name Trisha, I am overcome with good thoughts, because I cannot separate my wife from her name. A whole flood of emotions, experiences, joys, and desires comes to me at the sight or sound of those six letters put together in that name.

Names are precious, which is why we don't like our name ridiculed, twisted, or made fun of. I have a name that is fairly difficult to malign. With the middle name "Lee," some people have called me "Heavenly Kevinly," but that's hardly an insult. The worst name to stick is the name my friends in seminary gave me. Although "DeYoung" is a common Dutch name, apparently it was unfamiliar in Massachusetts, because people there would meet me and think my last name was Dion. So to this day my seminary friends call me Celine. Some friends! It's the only nickname I've ever had. Not the best I could hope for, but my heart will go on.

But funny nicknames given to us is one thing; irreverent use of God's name is another. Everywhere in Scripture the name of the Lord is exalted in the highest possible terms. "O LORD, our Lord, how majestic is your name in all the earth!" (Ps. 8:1a). "Ascribe to the LORD the glory due his name" (Ps. 29:2a). The first petition of the Lord's Prayer is "Hallowed be your name" (Matt. 6:9). The apostles proclaimed that "there is no other name under heaven given among men by which we must be saved" (Acts 4:12). Paul assured the Romans that "everyone who calls on the name of the Lord will be saved" (Rom. 10:13). And the culminating event in all of creation is when, "at the name of Jesus every knee should bow, in heaven and on earth and under the earth, and every tongue confess that Jesus Christ is Lord, to the glory of God the Father" (Phil. 2:10–11). The Bible does not want us to forget the holy importance of the divine name.

The *How*

This brings us back to the commandment itself. We've seen what the commandment meant in Israel and why it matters so much to God. Now, in this final section, we want to consider how we can obey the commandment in our own lives. Let's get at the application by focusing on what we should *not* do. There are three points: we violate the third commandment when we take up the name of God in service of (1) what is false, (2) what is frivolous, or (3) what is phony.

Violation 1: God's name in service of what is false. Whenever we attach God's name to lies, half-truths, or ill-conceived purposes, we break the third commandment. This means perjury is a serious sin because under oath we swear to "tell the truth, the whole truth, and nothing but the truth, so help me God." We also profane God's name by accusing him of things that are false. There is certainly a right, scriptural way to lament and cry out: "My God, my God, why have you forsaken me?" But to be angry with God, or (as some will tell you) to forgive God, as if he had sins or crimes against you, is to call into question his works and character and so to profane his name.

Maybe this will hit closer to home: if we use the name of God to ascribe a false sense of authority to our ideas, plans, or opinions, we violate the third commandment. Take politics for example. We ought to be very sure that the Bible speaks clearly about our preferred political policy or our newest cultural hot take before we insist that every Christian must agree with us. Likewise, we must be careful not to throw around phrases like, "God told me to do this," or "God wants us to do that." I understand that some Christian traditions use this sort of language casually, without trying to claim divine authority for every decision, but we shouldn't slap the name of God on the back of our plans just because we feel strongly about our proposed ideas.

I've always tried to keep this in mind when leading the church. When we were in the middle of a capital campaign and the elders found an existing church to buy and renovate, we were careful not to overstate our case. It would have been easy to say, "We've prayed about this and God has provided an open door. God wants us to have this building. But we need you to give generously. Will you be obedient to the Lord as we follow him?" Church leaders say that sort of thing all the time, and it's not fair. We can't claim divine authority for a capital campaign. What we can say is, "We've sought the Lord and spent a lot of time researching all the options. As your leaders, we all feel that this is the right move for the church, and we think God will be honored if we move forward together." The difference between the two speeches is subtle but significant. Phil Ryken puts it well:

> A more serious way to break the third commandment is by using God's name to advance our own agenda. Some Christians say, "The Lord told me to do this." Or worse, they say, "The Lord told me to tell you to do this." This is false prophecy! God has already said whatever he needs to say to us in his Word. Of course, there is also an inward leading of the Holy Spirit. But this is only an inward leading, and it should not be misrepresented as an authoritative word from God.[2]

When we claim absolute divine authority for our human plans and decisions, we violate the third commandment. God's name is holy, and it must not be added willy-nilly to our prudential decisions, no matter how sincere or important the decision might be.

Violation 2: God's name in service of what is frivolous. We also break the third commandment when we use the Lord's name carelessly. Jesus himself warns against vain repetition: "And when you pray, do not heap up empty phrases as the Gentiles do, for they think that they will be heard for their many words" (Matt. 6:7). Jesus is not trying to frighten new Christians or little kids who are just learning to pray. They are bound to be inarticulate at first (as many of us are years later!). Jesus's concern is not for polish of speech but for purity of heart. He doesn't want us to think that we get more prayer points for piling up pious phrases.

While the main point is to avoid showy prayers, there is surely some application for sloppy prayers too. After all, Jesus tells us to avoid *empty* phrases. I imagine we've all heard prayers that use the names and titles of God in a thoughtless way. We've all probably heard prayers made in this way: "Dear God, we just come to you, God. Lord, you're so awesome. Father, you died on the cross, Lord, and we just can't help but love and praise you for filling our hearts, Holy Spirit." Not only do prayers like this make a mess of the Trinity; they use the Lord's name as if it were little more than a breath or a comma. We ought to be more careful.

The same thing applies to praying with our kids around the dinner table or before bed. I know I've been convicted of this sin before. In the midst of freewheeling chaos, I'll quickly pray to God for the food or for the day and then be done. The problem is not a short prayer. The problem is that I am thoughtlessly tossing out the name of God as just one more hurdle to clear before we can eat or finally get some peace and quiet. No doubt God is more patient with three-years-olds who can't sit still than he is with parents who can't slow down to get their minds and hearts in the right place. It would be better not to pray over the meal at all, if the alternative is breaking the third commandment.

Using the Lord's name in a frivolous way would certainly include using "God" or "Jesus Christ" as curse words. Granted, modern cursing is somewhat different from Old Testament cursing, which was more like deliberate blasphemy than a bad habit. But, still, it says something about our attitude toward God if we can speak his name so lightly and carelessly. We're talking about our Creator, our Savior, our Judge, and our King. The God of the universe—the one Who Is That He Is—should not have his name tossed out flippantly as an expression of shock, outrage, or anger.

My parents were always careful about this, and I'm grateful for their caution. We couldn't say "Jeez" because it was short for "Jesus." We were never allowed to say "God" or "Gosh" or even "Oh my!" because they thought it was shorthand for "Oh my God." We may draw the line at different places when it comes to certain slang, but hopefully we all see the importance of protecting the honor of the Lord's name. When I hear Christians habitually rattle off "Oh my God!" for everything from a home run to a great parking spot, I can't help but wonder if they've not been well taught or if they don't know what God is really like.

And cursing isn't the only way to misuse the Lord's name. We must never use God's Word or name as a means to satisfy our ambition or avarice. I'm thinking of people who peddle the Word of God for profit, people who write Christian books or speak at Christian conferences or sing Christian music in order to get rich. Shame on them (or me!) if we use God's name as a means for our great gain.

Likewise, a joking, lighthearted approach to the Lord's name is inappropriate. This is one aspect of the third commandment I've thought about a lot. I like to crack jokes. I like to laugh. And I think it's fine, and probably healthy, that we can laugh at the silly things Christians do or the funny stereotypes about our churches. But using the name of Christ as a punchline is a different matter entirely. I fear many Christians are far too casual in telling jokes that have God in the midst of them. Would you casually make jokes about 9/11 or Auschwitz? Of course not. We understand that some things must be set apart. Some things are off-limits. Surely that's the case with God's name.

There is no place for using "Jesus Christ" in flippant humor or irreverent sloganeering. I remember seeing a Christian T-shirt, playing off the familiar beer advertising slogan, that said "This blood's for you." Someone was too clever for his own good. Or what about our use of Christian words and phrases in sarcastic ways? Like breaking into the "Hallelujah Chorus" when our team scores a touchdown. Or spilling our coffee and saying with a smirk, "Thank you, Jesus." Or making people laugh with our purposefully ill-timed "Praise the Lamb!" interjection. There are better ways to be silly than with such serious things.

Violation 3: God's name in service of that which is phony. Finally, if we can break the third commandment be being false or frivolous, we can also violate the commandment by being phony. Think about our approach to worship. Granted, we are all human, and we all get distracted. That's bound to happen. But that doesn't mean we shouldn't be careful to really mean the words we are singing or praying. When I was in college I sang in a first-rate choir with lots of music majors more talented than I. We sang stunningly beautiful pieces of choral music, almost all of which put biblical truths to music. And yet I know that many people in the choir cared nothing about the words they were singing, or even opposed the truths we were supposed to be celebrating. I suppose they viewed the pieces as art rather than as sacred music, but words are words, and we shouldn't sing what we don't mean.

Similarly, I wonder how many politicians mean it when they say, "God bless you, and God bless America." It may seem like an innocent expression of civil religion, but as Christians we know that the name of God is not something to toss around lightly or in an effort to win votes. We should never use the Lord's name in a perfunctory or trite manner.

Most importantly, as Christians, we sin every time we besmirch the name by which we're called. We must act, think, feel, and speak in a way that's proper for those who are called by the holy name of God. This is the point the Lord makes again and again in Ezekiel 36, announcing to his people that he will act on their behalf for the sake of his holy name, that they would no longer profane his name among the nations (vv. 16–23). We see the same thing in 2 Chronicles 7:14, where the Lord promises to hear the prayers of the people who are called by his name.

We must never forget the privilege and responsibility that comes with bearing the name of Christ. Sometimes you meet Christians who insist, "I'm a Jesus follower," or "I'm a disciple of the Messiah," or "I'm a Jesus person," or "I'm a follower of the way." They'll do anything to avoid saying the word *Christian*. And I understand that. The word can come with a lot of baggage. But it's our family name. It's the name that speaks of our union with God's Anointed One. We should not be ashamed of the name *Christian*. Nor should we be ashamed of the triune name in which we were baptized. Among other things, baptism is a naming ceremony. It's where we are marked out as belonging to the one God—Father, Son, and Holy Spirit. Consequently, we violate the third commandment when we, as baptized Christians, live as if we did not bear the name of God.

The worst thing that can be phony about us is us. That may be where some of us are. We go to church. We sing the songs. We say the right things. But it's not reality. Listen, if we are called by the holy name of God, we must not sully that name by living as if our conduct does not concern him or his glory.

If you want a simple summary of the third commandment—a New Testament exhortation putting in positive language all that is required of us—here it is: "Whatever you do, in word or deed, do everything in the name of the Lord Jesus, giving thanks to God the Father through him" (Col. 3:17). We obey the third commandment by living as Christians, by speaking and doing everything according to the family name. For when we do all that we do—and do it in Christ, for Christ, and through Christ—we show that his is the name we value, the name we love, and the name that is above all names.

4

Rest, Rejoice, Repeat

Remember the Sabbath day, to keep it holy. Six days you shall labor, and do all your work, but the seventh day is a Sabbath to the LORD your God. On it you shall not do any work, you, or your son, or your daughter, your male servant, or your female servant, or your livestock, or the sojourner who is within your gates. For in six days the LORD made heaven and earth, the sea, and all that is in them, and rested on the seventh day. Therefore the LORD blessed the Sabbath day and made it holy.

Exodus 20:8–11

The fourth commandment can be confusing.

Every one of the Ten Commandments is still binding, and every one has been deepened and transformed by the coming of Christ, this commandment more noticeably than the others. This is why Christians have not always agreed on how to obey the fourth commandment, or on whether the commandment needs to be kept at all.

Even within the Reformed tradition there are different understandings of what it means to observe the Sabbath, or honor the Lord's Day, or if these two expressions, Sabbath and Lord's Day, mean the same thing. Here's what the Westminster Confession of Faith says:

> [God] hath particularly appointed one day in seven, for a Sabbath, to be kept holy unto him: which, from the beginning of the world to the resurrection of Christ, was the last day of the week; and, from the resurrection of Christ, was changed into the first day of the week, which, in Scripture, is called the Lord's Day, and is to be continued to the end of the world, as the Christian Sabbath.[1]

Later, the Westminster Confession says that the day is to be set aside from all "worldly employments and recreations."[2]

The Heidelberg Catechism hits on similar themes but with a different emphasis. The catechism asks, "What is God's will for you in the fourth commandment?" The answer contains two parts:

> First, that the gospel ministry and education for it be maintained, and that, especially on the festive day of rest, I diligently attend the assembly of God's people to learn what God's Word teaches, to participate in the sacraments, to pray to God publicly, and to bring Christian offerings for the poor.

> Second, that every day of my life I rest from my evil ways, let the Lord work in me through his Spirit, and so begin in this life the eternal Sabbath.[3]

The Heidelberg Catechism does less to stress the Sabbath–Lord's Day connection, choosing instead to focus on corporate worship and resting from evil deeds.

And then there's this from the twenty-fourth chapter of the Second Helvetic Confession (1566), a document from the Swiss Reformation and one of the most popular and comprehensive statements of faith in the sixteenth century:

> We see that in the ancient churches there were not only certain set hours in the week appointed for meetings, but that also the Lord's Day itself, ever since the apostles' time, was consecrated to religious exercises and to a holy rest; which also is now very well observed by our churches, for the worship of God and the increase of charity. Yet herein we give no place unto the Jewish observation of the day, or to any superstitions. For we do not account one day to be holier than another, nor think that mere rest is of itself acceptable to God. Besides, we do celebrate and keep the Lord's Day, and not the Jewish Sabbath, and that with a free observation.[4]

All three documents talk about rest and worship on the Lord's Day. They all believe in the fourth commandment. But after that, there are some important differences. Is Sunday the Christian Sabbath? Or is it a festive day of rest? Or do we keep the Lord's Day, not the Sabbath, and "that with a free observation"?

Confusing, but Critical

If the fourth commandment can be confusing and controversial, that doesn't mean it's less important. In fact, you can make the case that the Israelites would have understood the fourth commandment to be the most important of the ten. For starters, it is the longest and most detailed commandment. Moreover, Sabbath observance is mentioned more often than any of the other Ten Commandments—eleven times in the Pentateuch and over one hundred times in the Old Testament. The Sabbath is the only other day in the Jewish calendar besides the Day of Atonement where all work is strictly prohibited, and the fourth commandment is the only one of the ten which the Lord clearly gave to the nation of Israel before they reached Mount Sinai (see Exodus 16). Even if we conclude that there are significant points of discontinuity between the Jewish Sabbath and the Christian Lord's Day, we would be unwise to suggest that God is indifferent to the principles of rest and worship.

When people think of the fourth commandment, they quickly jump to practical questions of scrupulosity: Can I go out to eat on Sunday? Can I watch football on Sunday? Do I have to take a nap on Sunday? But those are not the questions we should start with (and maybe they're not the questions we should end with either). I'll finish with three ways we can observe the fourth commandment. But first I want to provide a biblical overview of the Sabbath and try to sum up the moral principles inherent in Sabbath keeping.

The Sabbath in the Old Testament

Like so much theology, a proper understanding of the Sabbath begins in Genesis. We read in Geneis 2:3 that "God blessed the seventh day and made it holy." The Sabbath principle, therefore, was not invented by Moses after the exodus. It can be argued that the Mosaic Sabbath is not identical to the creation Sabbath, but it cannot be denied that we see a Sabbath principle at work from the very beginning of the world.

Have you ever thought about where the week comes from? Days come from the earth's rotation on its axis. Months are more or less gauged to the lunar cycle. The year is a result of the earth's revolution around the sun. In other words, scientific phenomena have given us days, months, and years. But why weeks? A seven-day week seems arbitrary, relative to the natural rhythms of the solar system. The week is what it is because God made it that way. He accomplished his work in six days and then rested on the seventh. Every time and everywhere we cycle through Sunday-Monday-Tuesday-Wednesday-Thursday-Friday-Saturday, we are embodying the Sabbath principles introduced into the world by God himself.

The church calendar is fundamentally a weekly calendar. I have no problem celebrating Good Friday, Easter, and Christmas. There are good historical and cultural reasons (along with gospel reasons) for highlighting these events each year. But the only calendar God gave to the church is the seven-day calendar that culminates in a day of worship and rest.

Exodus 20:8 calls us to *"remember* the Sabbath day," suggesting that the Sabbath was not being called into existence at Mount Sinai. *Remember* is more than a mental word in the Bible. It means to recollect and put into practice. To "remember the Sabbath day" was to acknowledge the sabbath principle in creation and own it for yourself. Interestingly, the parallel account of the Ten Commandments in Deuteronomy 5 roots the Sabbath in Israel's freedom from slavery. There it says, "Remember that you were a slave in the land of Egypt" (Deut. 5:15). The Sabbath, then, is grounded in both creation and redemption. It is a sign of God's creative purposes and saving grace.

The rest of the Old Testament helps us see how the fourth commandment took shape in ancient Israel. In Exodus 31 we see that the Sabbath became a sign of the Mosaic covenant. Just as a rainbow in the sky spoke of God's promise to Noah, so the Sabbath was the sign that God would take care of his people if they learned to trust him. Trusting the Lord meant resting from business as usual on the Sabbath (Isaiah 58; Amos 8) and gathering for a sacred assembly (Lev. 23:3). These were the twin engines of the Sabbath: worship and rest. The two were inextricably linked in the Old Testament. We rest so that we might be free to worship God; and we give God worship, in part, by trusting him enough to rest.

The Sabbath in the New Testament

As we turn our attention to the New Testament, it's important to note that we never see Jesus violate the fourth commandment. To be sure, he has no problem breaking with the traditions built upon the Sabbath, but his conflicts with the scribes and the Pharisees were not over the legitimacy of the Sabbath command itself. In Mark 2 Jesus approves of his hungry disciples picking heads of grain, noting that the Sabbath was made for man, not man for the Sabbath (v. 27). In Mark 3 Jesus heals a man with a shriveled hand, suggesting that we ought to do good on the Sabbath. In Luke 13 Jesus restores a woman with a disabling spirit, suggesting that the Sabbath is a day of freedom (v. 12). In Luke 14 Jesus heals a man suffering from dropsy, suggesting that the Sabbath is a day for mercy. To be sure, Jesus did not hesitate to peel away some of the accretions that were weighing down the Sabbath. More importantly, he reintroduced the Sabbath as a day for doing good, not just for doing our ritual duty. But the Gospel writers are at pains to demonstrate that Jesus never violated the fourth commandment (Matt. 5:17–18).

If Jesus tweaked the Jewish understanding of the Sabbath, Paul goes a step further in reconstituting a proper attitude toward the Mosaic Sabbath. In Romans 14 Paul is talking about *adiaphora* in the church, issues that Christians can agree to disagree on. Surprisingly, Paul puts Jewish holy days in this category:

> One person esteems one day as better than another, while another esteems all days alike. Each one should be fully convinced in his own mind. The one who observes the day, observes it in honor of the Lord. The one who eats, eats in honor of the Lord, since he gives thanks to God, while the one who abstains, abstains in honor of the Lord and gives thanks to God. (Rom. 14:5–6)

In the early church Jews and Gentiles had to figure out how to live together. It's no wonder there were disagreements about many of the Jewish rituals. What about the good laws? What about holy days? What were they to do with these aspects of Mosaic worship? Paul says, in effect, "Don't judge each other over these things. Christ has fulfilled certain aspects of the law. Some people will honor the special days; that's fine. Other people will choose not to honor the special days; that's fine too."

Paul says much the same thing in his letter to the Colossians. He's talking about the old written code, which has been nailed to the cross. He's talking about the aspects of the Mosaic law that have been fulfilled in Christ:

> Therefore let no one pass judgment on you in questions of food and drink, or with regard to a festival or a new moon or a Sabbath. These are a shadow of the things to come, but the substance belongs to Christ. (Col. 2:16–17)

How do we understand the fourth commandment in light of Paul's instructions in Romans 14 and Colossians 2?

I grew up in a home with strict Sabbath observance, and although I grumbled at the time, I'm thankful that my parents took Sunday very seriously. We went to church morning and evening. We went to Sunday school. We didn't play outside. And we never, ever mowed the lawn. We steadfastly avoided work (except my mom, it turns out, who had a tremendous feast to prepare every Sunday). I share my upbringing not because I've rebelled against it, but because my instinct is to want to prove that this kind of upbringing has the full weight of Scripture behind it.

And yet I can't avoid the conclusion, drawn from Romans 14 and Colossians 2, that we must be careful not to judge others for the sort of things Paul told us not to judge each other for! In hindsight, I'm not sure that every part of my upbringing was scrip-turally necessary—not wrong, but not required in every respect.

I know that some people have tried to argue that the Sabbaths mentioned here in Colossians 2 are a reference to monthly cel-ebrations, not weekly Sabbaths. But the record of the Old Testa-ment suggests otherwise. The threefold pattern—festivals, new moons, and Sabbaths—occurs several times: in the same order in Ezekiel 45 and in Hosea 2, and in a different order (but the same three things) in 2 Chronicles 8 and 31. In every instance, the three items seem to be shorthand for "annual holy days, monthly holy days, and our weekly holy day." I don't know how to make sense of the three items if "Sabbaths" means something other than the seventh day of the weekly Sabbath.

This means that there must be some important sense in which the Sabbath is no longer a binding holy day for New Testament Christians. Martin Luther, who was always good for an overstate-ment, once opined: "If anywhere the day is made holy for the mere day's sake—if anywhere anyone sets up its observance on a Jewish foundation, then I order you to work on it, to ride on it, to dance on it, to feast on it, to do anything that shall remove this encroach-ment on Christian liberty."[5] Luther may sound over the top, but he's not saying anything different in principle than we saw earlier in the Second Helvetic Confession.

But that's not all we need to say about keeping the fourth com-mandment. For there seems to be a deliberate attempt in the New Testament to reckon the Lord's Day as a new kind of Sabbath. Consider, for example, the account of the resurrection in the Gos-pels. In John 20, Luke 24, and Mark 16, the resurrection is said to have occurred "on the one of the Sabbath," usually translated "on the first day of the week." While the latter is a fair translation, the Greek word is actually "one," not "first." It appears, therefore, that the early church was already reckoning Sunday as the Sabbath day plus one. Christians would soon commemorate the eighth day of the week—the day of re-creation, the "one of the Sabbath."

This exegetical suggestion is made clearer in the rest of the New Testament and further developed in the early church. Acts 20:7 and 1 Corinthians 16:1–2 speak of the disciples gathering for worship on the first day of the week, while Revelation 1:10 refers specifically to the Lord's Day. From the second half of the early church's second century, it's clear that the term "Lord's Day" is being used for Sunday. Justin Martyr, the second-century apologist, said that the church met for worship on Sunday, the first day of the week. The Didache, a church manual from the early second century, used "the Lord's Day" to describe this day of corporate worship. The church father Ignatius, by the end of the first century, said "[Christians] no longer observe the Sabbath, but direct their lives toward the Lord's Day, on which our life is refreshed by him and by his death."[6]

If you look at the first four centuries of the church, you see that Sabbath keeping was spiritualized to mean a life of devotion and humility to God. Insistence on a strict observance of the seventh day was seen as Judaizing. In fact, the Council of Laodicea (363) went so far as to say that Christians should work on the seventh day and honor the Lord's Day instead.[7] Clearly there was a change afoot. As B. B. Warfield put it: "Christ took the Sabbath into the grave with him and brought the Lord's Day out of the grave with him on the resurrection morn."[8]

Putting It All Together

So how do we put this all together? Must we keep the fourth commandment or not? The short answer is, "Yes, but." Yes, we must keep the fourth commandment. It's part of God's revealed moral will for all people. But the way in which we keep the fourth commandment has changed.

Certain aspects of the Sabbath have been abolished. Strip away the cultural context and the case law, and the main takeaway from the Mosaic Sabbath is that we must rest from our labors and trust in God. This is the principle that we find fulfilled in Christ. Jesus showed us the fullest, deepest meaning of the Sabbath, namely, that we should trust in God to be our provider, sustainer, deliverer, and savior. The judicial penalties and ceremonial legalities of resting on Saturday have been eliminated.

Having said that, I believe key principles of Sabbath rest remain and were quickly appropriated for the Lord's Day. This was Calvin's position in the *Institutes*: "There is no doubt that by the Lord Christ's coming the ceremonial part of this commandment was abolished. . . . Christians ought therefore to shun completely the superstitious observance of days."[9] Calvin goes on to insist on the importance of observing the Lord's Day, maintaining that it was instituted as a substitute for the Sabbath and carries forward on the same principles. In particular, we still find that the Lord's Day is (1) a day to gather for worship, and (2) a day to rest from our labors. And, most importantly, the fourth commandment instructs us (3) to find our spiritual rest in Christ every day of the week.[10]

Let's look at each point in turn.

The Fitness of a Day for Worship

First, then, it is fitting that we set aside one day in seven for corporate worship. We've already seen this principle in both Testaments and in the early church. The first Christians inherited from their Jewish tradition the habit of gathering on a special day each week for prayer, fellowship, and instruction in the Word (Acts 2:42). That special day was Saturday under Moses but became Sunday in celebration of Christ's resurrection.

I've been a pastor for more than fifteen years now, and in those years I fear that I've seen regular Christians treat weekly worship less and less seriously. I grew up with my parents' unswerving commitment to morning and evening worship (and Sunday school and youth group and Wednesday night). Now that I'm a parent, I see how much effort it took to establish such a pattern. I'll always be thankful for the ingrained habit of going to church virtually no matter what. Are we teaching our kids that Sunday is the day we go to church or the day we try to squeeze in church? I understand that parents may draw the line in different places, but surely there are few habits more important to pass on to our children than the rock-solid routine of going to church every Sunday. It will be hard for our children to come to the conclusion that church is important for them if we raised them to think it was only a third or fourth priority for us. We may say that "Jesus is Lord" but end up showing that soccer is the real king.

Too many see corporate worship as a good thing to do if the weather is nice but not too nice; if the football game is uninteresting, and the sports practice doesn't interfere; or if they're not too tired. Somehow we've gotten the idea that gathering with God's people to worship at God's throne and to hear from God's Word is something that's fine to do when it fits in our schedule. This is not the New Testament ideal (Heb. 10:25).

I've often thought of this question for me and my children: Is Sunday my day of climax or collapse? For many of us, Friday and Saturday are climax, with dinners and parties and games and late nights out. Sunday is the day we try to get through as we get ready for Monday. If we are going to make the Lord's Day a day of worship instead of weariness, we need to plan ahead. We need to work hard on Saturday in order to listen well on Sunday.

Sunday is the day that the Lord has given you to attend to your soul. On Sunday you can do the good things that you have been meaning to do. You can read that Christian book, spend time in your Bible, go on a walk, pray, sing with your kids (and yes, take a nap!). If you were physically sick and didn't know what was wrong, you would go to doctors, set up appointments, check the Internet, call your insurance company, and read up on all the latest treatments. You would go far and wide seeking a remedy for your physical illness. But when it comes to spiritual illness, we barely look for a diagnosis, let alone the cure. Yet here is God, the Great Physician, saying, "I'll give you one day in seven to attend to your soul, to come and worship, to grow, to breathe, and to be nourished." Why would the day of worship not be a day of great gladness for us?

Trust Christ Enough to Rest

Second, we ought to trust Christ enough to stop and rest. The Sabbath was meant to be a day of gladness, not of gloom. But, sadly, God's people have not always seen it as such. "When will the new moon be over, that we may sell grain?" the people asked in Amos's day. "And the Sabbath, that we may offer wheat for sale" (Amos 8:5). God's people viewed the Sabbath as a day of restriction rather than a day of blessing, just as do kids who moan about taking a nap or adults who complain about the offices and restaurants that are closed on Sunday.

Granted, Christians have been overzealous in protecting the Lord's Day. In New England there were thirty-nine pages of small-print Sabbath laws in the days of the Pilgrims. John Owen once said, "A man can scarcely in six days read over all the duties that are proposed to be observed on the seventh."[11] Some people—though fewer than there used to be—may have bad experiences with forced scrupulosity on Sunday, but we shouldn't let too many rules lead us in the opposite direction of too little rest. Don't forget: the Sabbath was made for man, not man for Sabbath. Or as Ben Patterson put it, "What do we lose when we lose the Sabbath? We lose grace."[12]

When I was in college and seminary, I made what was a bold decision at the time and committed, along with a friend, that we would not do homework on Sundays. No reading assignments. No papers. No studying for tests. It meant rethinking my Saturdays, which meant being more thoughtful about my Friday evenings. I couldn't sleep until noon on Saturday, watch football, hang out with my friends all day, and go out to a social event at night and then play catch-up on Sunday. I had to make pretty drastic changes. But I never regretted the commitment. Setting aside Sunday was a habit that served me well all throughout my studies. Sunday became my favorite day of the week. I was freed up to go to church more than once. I could go on a long walk or read a book or take a nap. The day became an island of get-to in an ocean of have-to.

How many of us think, "You know what? Life is a little underwhelming. I'm not very busy. I wish the days could be more crowded. I wish life could be more hectic." Very few people think that way. So don't you want a day where you can say no to many of the oughts in your head? Wouldn't it be wonderful to have a day of freedom, one day in seven where the other six days have no claim on you?

Sabbath is the Hebrew word for "ceasing." It is the ceasing day—the stopping day. In an agrarian society, resting meant, "Sit down and don't worry about the fields." For many of us with desk jobs, resting might mean, "Go on a walk, ride your bike outside, and don't answer any emails!" Sabbath was not bondage, and the Lord's Day shouldn't be either. Can you imagine what good news the Sabbath was for slaves? After oppression for centuries, God says, "I give you one day in seven to worship and rest." Maybe God understands that we won't stop and rest unless he commands us to.

The Lord's Day is the first day of a new week. It's the eighth day. It's not the day of recreation per se, but of re-creation: to cease from what is necessary and embrace what gives life. We're not just vacating or evacuating, but re-creating. Let us not approach Sunday by saying, "How much can I get away with?" Instead, think, "What blessing does God mean to give me in worship and rest on this Lord's Day?" If the Sabbath principle is rooted in creation, taught in the Ten Commandments, and reasserted by Jesus, maybe we ignore the day at our peril. Not because God is frowning over us every time we break a sweat on Sunday, but because he means to smile over us with the blessing of worship and rest. After all, God made the Sabbath for man, not man for the Sabbath.

Cease from Works and Rest in Christ

Of the three Sabbath principles that remain, this is perhaps the most explicit and important: we keep the fourth commandment by resting in the finished work of Christ. This is the point the inspired author is making in Hebrews 4. There was a rest that God wanted his people to inhabit. And yet, in their rebellion, some of them never entered it. In his wrath, God swore that his disobedient people would not enter his rest (Heb. 4:3). But for those who believe, "there remains a Sabbath rest for the people of God" (v. 9). Therefore, we must—in a wonderful but biblically consistent sort of irony—strive to enter that rest (v. 11). And how do we do that? By resting from our works as God did from his (v. 10). This is the Sabbath rest that remains (and finds weekly expression in observing the Lord's Day): that we trust in Christ, believe in Christ, and rely on Christ instead of on our own strength.

God has always graciously given his people rest. We see it in creation. We see it at the palms of Elim. We see it in Joshua. We see it in David's day. We still see it today. "Come to me, all who labor and are heavy laden, and I will give you rest" (Matt. 11:28). The most important way we observe the Sabbath is by ceasing from our flawed, sinful labors and trusting in Christ alone for salvation.

Do we still need to obey the fourth commandment? Yes! Jesus says that he didn't come to abolish the Law and the Prophets, but to fulfill them (Matt. 5:17). So we obey the commandment but also recognize that Jesus has transformed it, and this commandment more than the others. Christ gives us the substance instead of the shadow. The Sabbath principle from creation to exodus to the New Testament Lord's Day has always pointed in the direction of trust. That's what the Sabbath has, at heart, always been about. Can you trust God to give you manna for two days on the sixth day? Can you trust God to make up for "lost" work on one day by blessing you on the other six days? Can you trust that this burden you're carrying is not yours to carry alone? Can you trust God to carry it (and carry you!) if you have faith enough to stop striving and start worshiping?

Resting can be hard work, whether we are talking about one day in seven or depending on Christ every day of our lives. That's why we must *strive* to enter God's appointed rest. We have to fight the fight of faith. We have to depend on God instead of our own planning and hard work. Sabbath rest is about making Jesus Christ the center of who we are. It means ceasing to find approval in others, stopping the foolish quest for our own righteousness, and trusting that true health, strength, vitality, and freedom can be found only when we cease from our labors and rest in Christ.

Some of us are running like crazy, thinking, "Oh, God. Why don't you give me some kind of break?" And he says, "I made this day for you—not to punish you or keep you in bondage but to give you the freedom you so desperately need." Some of you are desperately seeking the rest that you have not found in Christ—or you've found it, but you frequently forget it and never stop working, cleaning, planning, plotting, fretting, fussing, worrying, and trying to prove yourself to your parents, spouse, kids, or the church. You've never really appropriated what it means to have grace. There's always something else you need to do to show the world that you're worth something—that you're valuable, loved, and okay.

You don't have to earn anything. You don't have to prove anything. The world does not depend on you. Your salvation does not depend on you. In an ultimate sense, your family does not even depend on you. Can you hear the sweet voice of Jesus say, "Come to me . . . and I will give you rest"? Take him at his word. Believe him. Trust him. Run to him. And then, every Resurrection Day, give expression to what you believe by giving him praise and giving yourself a break.

5

Honor to Whom Honor Is Due

Honor your father and your mother, that your days may be long in the land that the LORD your God is giving you.

Exodus 20:12

Exodus 31 tells us that Moses came down from Mount Sinai with two stone tablets. Even though we refer to them as the two tablets (or tables) of the law, they were almost certainly not divided into two. Rather, they were two copies of the same thing. This was typical for covenants in the ancient Near East. You'd have one for each party. You couldn't just throw it onto a copy machine, so you had to bang it out on two different pieces of stone. One copy went into the ark of the covenant for the Lord, but the other was for them to remember.

Technically, then, the two tables of the law were the same table. But historically Christians have thought of one table for our vertical obligations to God and the other table for our horizontal obligations to our neighbor. There is evidence that the Jews and early Christians thought somewhat along these same lines. In the New Testament there are several places where only the commandments of the second table are listed, such as when Jesus talks to the rich young ruler in the Gospels. Also, in Romans 13 and 1 Timothy 1, there are step-by-step progressions through the different commandments of the so-called second table of the law. Jesus seems to operate with this understanding when he says:

> You shall love the Lord your God with all your heart and with all your soul and with all your mind. This is the great and first commandment. And a second is like it: You shall love your neighbor as yourself. On these two commandments depend all the Law and the Prophets. (Matt. 22:37–40)

This fifth commandment, then, is a transition from the first table to the second. If the foundation for the first table was the first commandment, then the foundation for the second table is the fifth commandment. We might not think of it in that way, but it's certainly the case. "Honor your father and mother" is the foundation upon which love for our neighbor is built.

The parental relationship is the first and most important relationship. It shapes all other relationships. When you come across a kind, considerate, capable student in your class (if you're a teacher in high school or a student in college), or come across someone in your workplace who seems hardworking, conscientious, responsible, and considerate, more often than not, you owe a great debt of gratitude to that person's parents. Now, there are all sorts of exceptions: good parents with bad kids, and bad parents with good kids. But, in general, that's the way the world works—the way that God has set up and designed things.

In this relationship with our parents, we learn what it is to have someone in authority over us, to listen to people, to honor them, and to do things that we sometimes don't want to do. Someone else has a say over us, so we're going to trust that they know better. Augustine said, "If anyone fails to honor his parents, is there anyone he will spare?"[1] This is where we learn to live with other people. This is where we learn that there are authority structures in the world. The family is where we learn about respect and obedience and hopefully (if it is a good family) about love and protection.

It is no wonder that when totalitarian regimes throughout history have tried to exert control over people, one of the chief mechanisms by which they've done so is severing that attachment to the family—making allegiance to the state the building block of society rather than the honoring of parents. The power of the state and the power of the family are often inversely related: one goes up as the other goes down.

I don't want to dwell on that macro point, but I do want us to see that the fifth commandment is bigger than just saying, "Kids, take a bath when Mom and Dad tell you to take one." Civilizations, societies, cultures, and countries do not flourish apart from social order, trust, and mutual respect. All of that is meant to be taught and imbibed in the incubator of the family. It's not too much to say that loving your neighbor begins with listening to Mom and Dad.

Honor Is Heavy

"Honor your father and mother" is a serious commandment. Just listen to what Moses says later in the Pentateuch:

> If a man has a stubborn and rebellious son who will not obey the voice of his father or the voice of his mother, and, though they discipline him, will not listen to them, then his father and his mother shall take hold of him and bring him out to the elders of his city at the gate of the place where he lives, and they

shall say to the elders of his city, "This our son is stubborn and rebellious; he will not obey our voice; he is a glutton and a drunkard." Then all the men of the city shall stone him to death with stones. So you shall purge the evil from your midst, and all Israel shall hear, and fear. (Deut. 21:18–21)

I'd bet they would hear and fear! To be sure, we live in the New Testament economy of salvation. All of these civil infractions have now been transposed into church order, with structure, membership, and discipline. But we see here how serious this infraction was.

Incidentally, doesn't this passage in Deuteronomy give you a better sense for how scandalous and remarkable the story of the Prodigal Son is? He ran away. He was a glutton and a drunkard. Yet at the moment when the father should have presented him before the elders to be stoned, while he was yet a long way off, he ran to him and said, "This my son was dead, and is alive again; he was lost, and is found" (Luke 15:24). There is good news for wayward children.

We also see that cursing parents was deserving of death in Exodus 21, Leviticus 20, and Proverbs 20 and 30. As Calvin said, "Nature itself ought, in a way, to teach us this. Those who abusively or stubbornly violate parental authority are monsters, not men."[2] Do your kids want to dress up like a monster for Halloween? All they have to do is not listen to their parents. There's a real monster. If they don't recognize those whose efforts brought them into the light of day, Calvin argued, they aren't worthy of its benefits. That was a different time, and we have a different sort of attitude toward parenting today, but sometimes we need a voice from five hundred years ago to remind us of the seriousness of this commandment.

———

In tackling the fifth commandment, I want us to look at four questions. First, what does it mean to honor our parents? Second, are there limits to honoring our parents? Third, why should we honor our parents? Fourth, what might it practically look like for us to honor our parents?

What Does It Mean to Honor Parents?

Calvin insists that honor requires three things: "reverence, obedience, and gratitude."[3] The reverence is not because our parents always are deserving of it in themselves. I write as a father who is very aware of his inadequacies and shortcomings. I've had many occasions where I've said, "I can't believe I just spoke or acted like that." It's not because we're always deserving of it that we must be honored, but because of the position of authority that God has granted to us. The word *honor* is the Hebrew word *kabod*. It's the Old Testament word for "glory" or "weight." To be a parent is a weighty thing. To be given the title of mother or father is to be designated with an office of great significance.

Obedience means that we do what our parents say while we're a part of their household. Even when we've grown and left the home, we make an effort to do their wishes whenever we can. Obedience, of course, implies that parents are giving commands and passing along instructions. We don't hope that children figure things out for themselves. We don't leave them to their own devices and find a way to be their best friend. No, we give them orders and expect obedience.

We don't have to be the only ones to give our kids instruction, but we are the responsible ones. No matter how you choose to educate your children—whether homeschool, public school, or Christian school—you are the one who is responsible to ensure that what they are learning is good and right and will help them to grow in Christ.

We'll come back to gratitude again at the end of the chapter—but kids, if you're reading, you need to know this about your parents. We really love to do nice things for you most of the time. We really do. We like to get you things and see you happy. We like to know that we've done something that gives you some sort of joy in life. You know what would be really nice? If you didn't forget it instantly. We've all had this experience as parents. You get up and say, "Hey, kids! Today is donut day! Get in the car. We're getting donuts!" We'd like to think that ought to carry over for a good five seconds. Of course, it's over before the sprinkles hit the floor. The kids are off to the next thing, but that's not the way it should be.

Gratitude is one of the chief ways we can honor our parents. I didn't understand when I was a kid, but the life of a parent is one of constant sacrifice. It's joyful, but it's a sacrifice of parents' money, time, energy, desires, sleep, and sometimes tears. It's an office and a responsibility of great sacrifice. One of the ways that we can show honor to those who have sacrificed so much for us is by simply being grateful.

Are There Limits to Honoring Parents?

Are there limits to honoring parents? In a word, yes. Authority can be abused. In Acts 5 we see a principle that has to do with government but also with parents, church leadership, and any other authority over us: if the choice is between obeying God or obeying men, we obey God. If your parents command you to do what God forbids or forbid what God commands, you cannot and must not obey your parents. One way to think of this is that the first table of the law takes precedence over the second. But even in those (hopefully rare) cases, there's still a way to be respectful and honor your parents—even if they're asking something of you that they don't have the authority to ask.

Parents should not expect the same obedience from grown children as they did when their children were young. We see a divine design in Genesis that Jesus later reiterates in Matthew 19: a man will leave his father and mother and cleave to his wife, and they will become one flesh. Even in the ancient world, where people often literally lived under the same roof, and would almost certainly have lived in very close quarters to one another, there was still a leaving and cleaving. A new unit was formed. With that newness came a severing of some of the old obligations. It wasn't an entire separation, but there was a change.

In our culture, where some people don't get married and where others marry later in life, I think that moving out of the home establishes that same kind of break. When the mom is fifty, she can't expect to call up her twenty-five-year-old daughter and tell her, "You must do this with your children. Here are all the things that you are doing wrong," and have her simply say, "Yes, I will obey." There are limits. The parental authority is not absolute.

But in most Western countries, our problem is not a knee-jerk obedience to parents. If we were to weigh out the greater danger on the scales, the danger is not, "I'm giving immediate deference to my parents. I'm not seeing the ways in which I need to break and establish my own identity." We have to realize that almost everything in our culture mitigates against this kind of respect. We don't have the sort of culture that says, "When you get older is when you're most wise and deserving of respect." What we have is, "When you get older, you should take a backseat. Youth culture equals pop culture, and pop culture equals whatever fifteen- to twenty-five-year-olds are into." Our culture tends not to honor the generations who have gone before.

Wouldn't it be wonderfully countercultural for people to step into a church and find the opposite? "Here is a place where we value age and look to the wisdom of our elders." As long as I am still somewhat counted among young people, I'm going to bang this drum so that people don't think, "You're just saying this because you want people to listen to you." No, I'm saying that you ought to listen to people who are a lot older than me. That's one of the things that I have tried to do as a pastor. I count it as one of my greatest privileges as a pastor that I've always served with elders who were old enough to be my dad—or maybe, when I started, my grandfather! They are men I can look up to and respect, no matter what degree or title I have. These men have gone farther in godliness than I have in many ways, and I ought to listen to and respect them.

We assume that it is the rite of passage for teenagers to rebel—that it's just what they do. But that's not just what they do. When they do, it's sinful. Yes, there is a natural development and progression of establishing one's own identity and figuring stuff out for oneself. You don't parent a fifteen-year-old the way that you parent a five-year-old. But let's not assume that these steps toward proper independence give us a license for rebellion, disrespect, stubbornness, or disobedience.

Why Should We Honor Parents?

Ephesians 6:1 says we are to obey our parents "in the Lord." It's part of our devotion to Jesus to honor our mom and dad. Sometimes young people come to Christ as teenagers or in young adulthood, but their parents weren't Christians (or weren't very serious Christians). Sadly, when they get on fire for the Lord, it can make them worse as a son or daughter. They return home thinking that they know everything that their parents never knew. Maybe we do know something about faith that our parents don't, but surely we don't want to show our unbelieving parents that becoming a Christian has made us less respectful and willing to honor them.

Instead, when children come home, their parents ought to say, "I don't know what happened to you at college this semester. You're talking about church all the time and wanting to read your Bible. It's a little weird. I think that you're a little carried away with this religion stuff. And yet I can't deny that you've changed. You're wonderful to be around. Maybe there is something to this God whom you profess to believe in." Our obedience and devotion to Christ lead to obedience to and honor for our parents.

Children are told to obey their parents in everything, for this pleases the Lord (Col. 3:20). By implication, not listening to our parents displeases the Lord. Even Jesus obeyed his parents—and he was perfect, and they were not! If you ever have a moment where you think, "I know so much more than my parents. In fact, I feel like I'm living life much better than my parents. I'm much closer to perfection than my parents"—congratulations, you're a lot like Jesus, and Jesus never disobeyed his parents.

> He went down with them and came to Nazareth and was submissive to them. And his mother treasured up all these things in her heart. (Luke 2:51)

I can understand. If my kids were submissive to me, I'd treasure that in my heart too! In all things, Jesus—the second person of the Trinity, perfect in all his ways—was submissive. When Mary or Joseph told him what to do, he did it!

A song we sing at Christmastime, "Once in Royal David's City," contains a verse that I've always thought was a little schmaltzy, but it's true:

> And, through all His wondrous childhood,
> He would honor and obey,
> Love and watch the lowly maiden,
> In whose gentle arms He lay:

> Christian children all must be
> Mild, obedient, good as He.[4]

That's always rubbed me the wrong way. The point of Christmas is not that he came down so that we could be good children like him. None of us will be as obedient as he was. Yet is there anything untrue in that line? He would honor and obey, and Christian children should be as he was. He is our example.

But what we see most explicitly here in Exodus 20:12 is that this is the first commandment with a promise, as the New Testament will tell us. In Ephesians 6 Paul gives a variation on the promise: "Honor your father and mother . . . that it may go well with you and that you may live long in the land" (vv. 2–3). When Exodus 20:12 says, "Honor your father and your mother, that your days may be long in the land that the LORD your God is giving you," it's not just about living a long time. The writers of the Bible were not dumb. They lived in a real world where people died. It wasn't like everyone who was really good lived to be one hundred years old, and everyone who was really bad died early. Living long in the land was more than just chronology. The phrase really has to do with abundant life. If you want to enjoy to the full the blessings that God has for you in the Promised Land, you'll listen to your mom and dad.

So, on the one hand, it's a reward, but it's more than that: it's a promise. It's not, "Hey, if I see ten obedience points today, you get an extra year of life!" No, it's a recognition of the way the world works—the way in which God has designed things. It's not a mathematical formula, but you will generally be much better off after learning to honor your parents.

Isn't it great how God motivates us to holiness? He could have just said, "Honor your father and mother, or else." Paul could have said it was "the first commandment with a big threat." But instead God said, "Let me lay this out for you. You're going to want to do

88

this. It's not within your sin nature to do it, but don't you want to live long in the land? Don't you want to experience blessing in life?" God gives us a path toward that end, and it starts as children with honoring mom and dad.

Anyone in the social sciences field, whether liberal or conservative, has to acknowledge that study after study has shown that the best predictor for health as an adult and for making it through school, staying out of jail, keeping off drugs, and avoiding promiscuity—and whatever other pattern of social benefit—is what happens in the home. Again, there are all sorts of exceptions that go better or worse than what the statistics say, but the best predictor is whether you had a mom and a dad who loved you and were there for you, and whether you listened to them and followed them. This is the way the world works.

Kids need parents—that is a biblical truth. And the very moment we think we don't need our parents is probably the moment we need them more than ever. When you're seven or eight, you don't even think about life without your parents. You need somebody to feed you. Then you grow up and get to a point where you think, "I don't know. Maybe I could do this on my own. Maybe what my friends want is a little more important. Maybe what they're doing is going to serve me better than what my parents think I should be doing." When you get to the point as a teenager that you think, "I don't really know that this is a relationship I need"—it's at that moment you need your mom and dad more than ever to love and encourage you, to set appropriate boundaries for you, and sometimes to guard you from your own impulses.

How Can We Obey This Commandment?

Let's get really practical. How can we obey the fifth commandment? For starters, we could say that the commandment is larger than just parenting. There's a long tradition of understanding this commandment (and all the commandments) as having a broad application. Christians have always understood that the fifth commandment is not just about parents and children but about that relationship as a template for any other relationship of authority we have in our lives.

The New Testament says that slaves ought to obey their masters—or, as we would say in our context, employees ought to listen to their employers. Wives are to submit to their husbands as to the Lord. Hebrews 13:7 says to obey our leaders in the church and submit to them. First Peter 5:5 says that younger men ought to be subject to the elders. Romans 13 says that we ought to be subject to the governing authorities. Titus 1:1 says to be submissive to rulers and authorities, obedient for every good work. First Peter 2:17 tells us to fear God and honor the king.

Thankfully, we live in a country where there is freedom of religion and of speech (at least for now). We have the right to speak out against our leaders if they are acting wickedly. We see this in the Old Testament. The prophets often denounced the kings. There is a place for this. In a republic we have an opportunity to effect change by affirming or criticizing those in leadership over us. Many of these criticisms are probably warranted. Yet we are to fear God and honor the king. We are to be subject to every governing authority, even the ones whom we didn't vote for or who we can't believe would get elected. We are subject to them. Even as we are critical of them, we must do so in a way that shows respect for the office and position that they have been granted— sometimes as a great means of grace and other times as a means of judgment.

Four Final Words

I want to close this chapter by giving you four simple things that you can say as a way to honor your father and mother.

The first thing you can say is: "Yes, Mom," or, "Yes, Dad." Prompt, cheerful obedience is a way to honor your father and mother. "Son, could you sweep up the floor?" "Yes, Mom." I can tell you that that would sound amazing! I'll even let you cheat: just a smile would be fine. Even not saying, "Ugh," would be a start! Don't say, "Ugh," or, "I didn't make the mess!" If you want to get your mom into one of her favorite lectures, try saying, "I didn't make this mess." Oh, boy, here she comes: "You want to talk about cleaning up messes you didn't make? Sit down for a moment!" Don't even go there. But that's one thing you can say: "Yes, Mom." Wow. That would be amazing.

The second thing you can say is: "Thank you, Dad," or, "Thank you, Mom." I love it when my kids say that. They're pretty good at doing it. I know that teaching like this is hard for some of us, because our relationship with our mom and dad is hard, or because they have long since passed away. But if you live with your mom and dad or still have them somewhere, it would be good to give them a call and say, "I just want to say thank you. I don't know if I've said it enough. I'm sure I didn't say it after all the meals, cooking, cleaning, and Christmas presents. So I just want to say thank you."

The third thing we can say is: "I'm sorry." This is probably even harder than the first two. Don't do what famous people do when they don't really mean it: "I'm sorry if you were offended." "I'm sorry, but what they did was worse." Just say, "I'm sorry. I shouldn't have done that. I knew better," or, "I didn't know better, but now I do."

Who knows what sort of healing might come to your parental relationships to simply say, "I'm sorry." If you have in your mind, "I know that it's 85 percent my parents' fault. They've never acknowledged or said anything. If I say, 'I'm sorry,' they're going to think that they never did anything wrong," then let the Holy Spirit do his work in their lives. The Holy Spirit is doing work in your life. Maybe he's bringing you to a point where you can say something you should have said years ago: "I'm sorry."

Finally, say, "Hello." Stop by. Pick up the phone. Send a picture. Try to text. Make a point to be there for the holidays, if you can. There is probably nothing that a mom and a dad—especially a mom—would like more in all the world than to see all their kids and grandkids in one place. Does it always happen? No, it can't always happen. But it means the world to a parent when you just say, "Hello." For some of us, that may be a start. Pick up the phone and say, "We haven't talked for a couple of weeks. How are you?" Even if you have to say, "I was reading this book, and the author told me I should call. So what do you want to talk about?" It's a start. Never stop saying, "Hello."

If you don't have children or living parents, or you don't even know who they are, you will please God—the God of families— by loving the family of God. In some ways, Jesus even relativizes the traditional family unit. He says, "My mother and my brothers are those who hear the word of God and do it" (Luke 8:21). This is why kinship terms are used so frequently in the New Testament church. Paul can say he's a spiritual father, and those to whom he writes are his children. We are his brothers and sisters. There are opportunities for all of us to follow these commandments. We have a heavenly Father to honor, and all the family of God to love and serve. For all of us, this is a good place to start.

6

Murder, We Wrote

You shall not murder.

Exodus 20:13

"You shall not murder." That's the entire sixth commandment. In Hebrew, it's actually even shorter—just two words, in fact: *lo*, the negation ("not"), and *ratsach*, "murder." It seems like an obvious, uncontroversial commandment. If any command could go unstated, any that we as human beings and good neighbors would simply assume, perhaps it would be this one. Surely people from all times and places could agree that we shouldn't murder.

But have you ever wondered why murder is wrong? Even if it's assumed to be wrong universally in the Western world, why is that the case? You could probably go out and talk with anyone in your town, and one hundred out of one hundred people would agree that murder is wrong. If you asked them why, they would probably say something like, "It's just not right." Or maybe they'd go a step further: "If our society is to function—if we're to feel safe and flourish as human beings—we can't just go around killing each other willy-nilly." When it comes down to it, most people would defend the rightness of this commandment by some form of utilitarian ethics. Why is murder wrong? Because that's just the way that things work.

But that leads to another question: who decides whether your life is worth protecting? Who's to say that your life being snuffed out wouldn't make the world a better place? As Christians we realize that the sanctity of life is based on more than pragmatic considerations. We know that every human being is created in the image of God (Gen. 1:26–27). No matter people's race or ethnicity, how they vote, their health or disabilities, their age or infirmities, or whether they are bothersome to others, every person has inherent worth and dignity, since each one is created to represent God. Biblical anthropology allows for the sixth commandment to be based on something deeper than utilitarianism and something better than good, practical advice.

———

I want to explore the sixth commandment by asking three questions: What does the sixth commandment prohibit? How does this commandment speak into our cultural context? And how does Jesus deepen and transform this commandment?

What Does the Sixth Commandment Prohibit?

Simply put, the sixth commandment prohibits taking innocent human life. The word *murder* is a good translation of the original Hebrew word, *ratsach*, which is used in the commandment. It's more accurate than the translation "to kill." The Hebrew word *ratsach* mostly occurs in the few passages in the Pentateuch that mention cities of refuge, places to which those who had committed unintentional manslaughter could flee before outraged friends and family members sought revenge. Outside of those few passages, *ratsach* does not occur very often. Comparatively, the Hebrew word *qatal*, "to kill," occurs hundreds of times. There is a difference between *ratsach* and *qatal*.

As we see in the Old Testament, the sixth commandment does not prohibit self-defense: "If a thief is found breaking in and is struck so that he dies, there shall be no bloodguilt for him, but if the sun has risen on him, there shall be bloodguilt for him" (Ex. 22:2–3). In other words, if someone had no other choice but to kill as a way to defend himself from an intruder, he was not guilty. But verse 3 adds, "If the sun has risen on him, there shall be bloodguilt for him," which means that if observers could see what was happening and could discern that killing wasn't necessary, the one who killed was guilty. Self-defense, then, is not a violation of the sixth commandment.

We see in Genesis 9 that capital punishment was also not considered a violation of the sixth commandment: "Whoever sheds the blood of man, by man shall his blood be shed, for God made man in his own image" (v. 6). Capital punishment for murder was not considered an assault on the image of God, but a defense of his image. Human life is so precious that the taking of it was to be punished severely.

The famous principle of *lex talionis*—"eye for eye, tooth for tooth, wound for wound," stated in Exodus 21, was not cruel and unusual punishment. Gandhi once said, "An eye for an eye makes the whole world blind," and we think, "Oh, that's right. That's not a very good law." But within the context of the ancient Near East, this was quite a humane law. It said, "An eye for an eye, a tooth for a tooth, and a wound for a wound," instead of, "Your head for an eye, your family for a tooth, and your tribe if you offend me." It set the precedent that the punishment must fit (and not exceed) the crime. Life for life—no less and no more. This is the same principle reiterated in Romans 13. The governing authorities are God's servant for good, an avenger to carry out God's wrath on the wrongdoer (v. 4). Capital punishment was not considered a violation of the sixth commandment.

Neither was war, in certain circumstances. Peace is always the goal, of course, but war is sometimes necessary to defend peace. The Old Testament clearly did not prohibit warfare, since God sent Israel into battle and claimed to be a warrior God who fought for them. Again, we see in Romans 13 that the duly appointed state is to be the agent of God's wrath and to protect the innocent. As you may recall, when Jesus encountered the centurion, he did not tell him, "Go and sin no more—and, if you're really going to follow me, quit being a centurion in the Roman army." In Acts, Cornelius (the head of a regiment) was called a God-fearer. When some soldiers asked John the Baptist what they needed to do to repent, John did not say: "Resign from the evil Roman army. You can't be a soldier and be part of the people of God." Instead he said, "Do not extort money from anyone by threats or false accusations. Be content with your wages. Be an honest, honorable soldier," even in an army that often did repugnant things, as the Roman army did (see Luke 3:14). So the sixth commandment did not prohibit that sort of killing—self-defense, capital punishment, and just wars.

But it did prohibit premeditated, intentional murder. We see this several times in the Old Testament such as in the murder of the Levite's concubine or wife and the murder of Naboth for his vineyard. It prohibited intentional but unpremeditated murder—what we would call "voluntary manslaughter." It prohibited reckless homicide, or involuntary manslaughter, such as someone who drives drunk and kills another. Although there was no intention to kill anyone, death occurred through recklessness. There was a distinction in Israelite law between accidental death and death motivated by hatred (Deut. 19:1–13). The Old Testament was wise in considering the intention behind the death.

The sixth commandment forbids negligent homicide:

> When you build a new house, you shall make a parapet for your roof, that you may not bring the guilt of blood upon your house, if anyone should fall from it. (Deut. 22:8)

> When an ox gores a man or a woman to death, the ox shall be stoned, and its flesh shall not be eaten, but the owner of the ox shall not be liable. But if the ox has been accustomed to gore in the past, and its owner has been warned but has not kept it in, and it kills a man or a woman, the ox shall be stoned, and its owner also shall be put to death. (Ex. 21:28–29)

At first, these laws sound sort of strange. Most of us don't go out in fear of oxen chasing us when we are on a walk. We're not worried about having parapets on our roof. But we have laws that require a fence around below-ground pools. We must protect people from falling into the pool, just like Israel was required to protect people from oxen and roofs. In that day, the way to get cool at night was to go out on the roof, which served as additional living space. God was saying that people had to care about their neighbor. They couldn't just say, "Well, you fell off the roof. It's your own fault." He commanded them to care about the well-being of their neighbor by putting a parapet around the roof. It was similar with the ox. If an ox went wild and chased people, it was an accident. But if the ox's owner knew that the ox was likely to go after people, and then the ox did so and gored someone, the owner hadn't been doing his part to care for his neighbor, and he was to be put to death.

We see, then, that the sixth commandment prohibits much more than just cold-blooded, premeditated murder. It prohibits killing or causing to be killed by direct action or inaction any legally innocent person. That's the answer to the first question.

How Does the Sixth Commandment Speak to Our Culture?

Certainly the sixth commandment applies to us in all the same ways. We still care about homicide, involuntary and voluntary manslaughter, and all these technical terms. In addition, though, let me highlight three related areas that are particularly relevant (and sometimes controversial).

The Sixth Commandment Prohibits Suicide

There is almost no topic more painful than suicide for those who have experienced it with family or friends. Suicide is a sin—not the unforgivable sin, but a sin. Of course, that's not what I would lead with as a pastor going to visit a family who just lost a loved one to suicide. I'm not talking about my pastoral care strategy at the moment, but giving you the doctrinal foundation.

There may be extreme cases where a suicidal person has clearly lost control over his or her faculties, such as certifiable dementia or closed head injuries. Such a person doesn't have any sort of capacity for rational decision making. But in the majority of cases, we are right to see suicide, as tragic as it is, as a morally culpable and blameworthy choice. For centuries the church has consistently viewed suicide as a violation of the sixth commandment, since self-murder is still murder.

There are five instances of suicide in Scripture: Judges 9:50–57; 1 Samuel 31:1–7; 2 Samuel 17:23; 1 Kings 16:15–19; and Matthew 27:3–10. All these suicides are in the context of shame and defeat. Likewise, when more noble characters ask God to take their lives (such as Jonah or Job), God clearly views their self-destructive requests unfavorably.

We hear far too often of famous movie stars, athletes, or entertainers who have committed suicide. Many people were understandably upset and saddened by Robin Williams's death. There was much conversation and punditry, and people said things in perhaps an unhelpful way or with unhelpful timing. But one of the recurring themes was a lack of moral responsibility: "We all have our demons. We all have to face this. We shouldn't put any sort of ethical blame on one who commits suicide."

Initially that sounds compassionate—but it isn't. Listen to a woman named Julie Gossack, who wrote for the *Journal of Biblical Counseling* ten years ago. She's a wife and a mother who has suffered through the suicides of five family members. I can scarcely imagine that. She said this:

> Suicide is not a genetic trait nor is it a family curse. Suicide is a sinful choice made by an individual. This statement is neither unloving nor disrespectful. It is the truth. I dearly loved my family members that committed suicide, but their choices were sinful and not righteous.[1]

She adds that she intends her words to be loving, so that other people in a dark place who might be considering taking their lives would, if there are no other restraints, perhaps be restrained by the law of God. Suicide might feel like the only way out, but Scripture tells us that God will never lead us into a situation where violating his commandments is the only option. We do not help struggling saints by refusing to tell them that suicide is displeasing to God. Lovingly spoken, in the right time, that may be one way in which God jolts the suicidal soul back to better, saner, more righteous thinking. Your life is precious to God, even when you have concluded that it's pointless.

The Sixth Commandment Prohibits Abortion

"For you formed my inward parts; / you knitted me together in my mother's womb" (Ps. 139:13). The psalmist is speaking here of the nascent life (which is truly life) within the mother. I already mentioned a law from Exodus 21: "Eye for eye" (v. 24). If you read the context there, it has to do with injuring a woman's baby while still in the womb. There were punishments for doing so, because that life was considered life. Until very recently the church has universally opposed abortion. The Didache says, "Do not murder a child by abortion or kill a newborn infant"—two practices that were common in the ancient world. It was chiefly in the Judeo-Christian worldview, particularly in the early church, that children were valued and considered to need protection. Commenting on Exodus 21:22–25, John Calvin writes:

> For the fetus, though enclosed in the womb of its mother, is already a human being, and it is almost a monstrous crime to rob it of the life which it has not yet begun to enjoy. If it seems more horrible to kill a man in his own house than in a field, because a man's house is his place of most secure refuge, it ought surely to be deemed more atrocious to destroy a fetus in the womb before it has come to light.[2]

Life begins at conception. That's a scientific fact. Any embryology book will tell you that the life of each one of us traces back to the zygote—to the moment of conception. We didn't become something different. We've all been formed from that original life, which is still us.

The only way to think that ending life in the womb is appropriate is to think that personhood begins at some time other than the beginning of biological life. And yet the Bible assumes—and, until very recently, everyone in the Western world agreed—that there is a profound and organic unity between body and soul, such that personhood exists wherever biological life exists. The ancient heresy Gnosticism posited a dualism whereby the physical body and the soul did not exist in organic unity. One was trapped inside the other and needed to be set free. But we understand from a biblical anthropology that, though they are two things, the body and the soul have an organic union. When your biological life begins, you also exist as a person made in the image of God, created to honor God, and with a life that deserves to be protected.

The Sixth Commandment Prohibits Euthanasia

Assisted suicide laws continue to make headway in America and in the rest of the Western world. Legal and medical experts point to a number of problems with the laws themselves. Some of these laws don't require notification of family members. They don't specify which kind of doctor must diagnose you. They also allow you to pick up your suicide drugs at your local pharmacy and administer them on your own. And that's to say nothing about doctors getting their terminal diagnoses wrong.

Just as important are the ethical problems with these laws. How can we try to prevent suicide among teenagers and young people and encourage it among the sick and elderly? I often see signs in high schools that read, "Say No to Suicide," or, "Thinking about Suicide? There is help." How can we promote that message to students and then put forward a very different message to the elderly? We are to do what we can to preserve and protect all innocent life.

We must not let foggy definitions of compassion cloud our thinking. This is the key distinction: we are not talking about the termination of treatment, but the termination of life. Sometimes people hear that spiel about suicide and say, "Look, I don't want to be put on a respirator. I don't want to have a machine do my life for me." That's not what euthanasia laws are about.

My grandfather passed away a couple of years ago at ninety-one years old. He went downhill very quickly. When he was in hospice care, he was told, "There are some things we can do. We can force you to get up and move around and give you some further treatments, and it might preserve your life for another four or five months. Or we can keep you comfortable, give you palliative care, and you can rest in your bed. You may not live more than a week or two." He said, "I'm ninety-one. I've lived my life. I want to rest. I don't need to do all that to preserve my life for four or five more months." Many of us face those decisions, and we know loved ones who've had to face them. Those decisions are not wrong. He was choosing to end treatment, not to end his life.

Assisted-suicide laws have consequences most people don't think about on the front end. The Netherlands was the first nation to allow legal assisted suicide, and over time they've seen the voluntary become involuntary. When it becomes an option for you to end your life, insurance companies say, "Well, we aren't going to pay for that treatment to extend your life another six months or a year. You can just take these pills and end your life." You become a burden to insurance providers, to the state, and to your family. More and more requests for assisted suicide in the Netherlands are coming from family members, not from the patients themselves. During the Nazi occupation of the Netherlands, Dutch physicians refused to obey orders by Nazi troops to let the elderly and the terminally ill die. In 2001 Holland became the first country to give legal status to doctor-assisted suicide. As Malcolm Muggeridge noted, it took only one generation to transform a war crime into an act of compassion.[3] Blessed are those who have regard for the weak (Ps. 41:1).

Every human life is precious. Unborn life is precious. Children with special needs are precious. Aging parents are precious—even when they don't remember because they're suffering dementia, they're still made in the image of God. Nonverbal children or parents, those in a wheelchair, and those who are completely dependent upon others or doctors are precious. All of life matters to God. If we have our eyes open, we can see this in even the most surprising places in the Bible, like in the *lex talionis* of the Mosaic law. You see it in *imago Dei*. You see it in the incarnation, when God entered the world as a helpless babe.

Defend, honor, and give thanks for life—yours, your children's, and your parents'. The sixth commandment means to protect it.

How Did Jesus Transform the Sixth Commandment?

I want to finish by moving from cultural analysis to heart analysis. In the Sermon on the Mount, Jesus deepens and transforms this commandment, helping us to understand its true significance. The sixth commandment not only prohibits violent acts of murder but all violent emotions and intentions of the heart (Matt. 5:21–26). You and I can be 100 percent murder free but still face the wrath of God if our life is marked by anger, bitterness, invective, insult, and rage.

In David Powlison's book *Good and Angry* he has a chapter entitled, "Do You Have a Serious Problem with Anger?" It's very clever, because the chapter is only one word long: "Yes."[4] That's all it says. And rightly so. You and I have an anger problem. And if we don't get it under control, we may be in danger of hell.

And that's not all Jesus says about anger. He gives two illustrations—one about going to the temple and one about going to court—and neither is about *our* anger. Jesus says that anger is so serious that we should not only do what we can to eliminate it in our heart, but also do what we can to prevent and alleviate it in others. The sixth commandment doesn't just forbid physical murder or even simply prohibit murder of the heart. It positively enjoins us to seek reconciliation.

Later in the Sermon on the Mount, Jesus will say that we are to love our enemies and pray for those who persecute us. Sociodemographic categories are all we hear in politics. Everyone is a category: white evangelicals, African Americans, Asian Americans, uneducated, working class, the 1 percent. Everyone gets a little category. Jesus says that if you love only the people who like you, dress like you, root for the things you do, and vote for the people you do—well, that's no big deal. Everybody does that. What about your enemies? What about the people who mistreat you? What about the people who don't understand you? By condemning envy, hatred, and anger, the Heidelberg Catechism says that God tells us to love our neighbors as ourselves, to be patient, peace loving, gentle, merciful, and friendly to them.[5]

Did you notice what Jesus said at the end of Matthew 5:26? He says that if you are this sort of angry fool, "you will never get out until you have paid the last penny." If you insist on pouring out the cup of your wrath, there's another cup for you to drink. As he is apt to do, Jesus makes the one commandment we would have thought we were all going to feel pretty good about into one of the commandments we all feel pretty bad about. Which one of us hasn't been unrighteously angry this week? There is a way to be righteous in anger, but that's not the way that most of us are angry. We show it in the way we speak to our spouse, when we silently judge, when we explode at our children over the simplest things, and when somebody drives in front of us and goes too slow, and you would think that they had cursed your whole family for all time. Jesus says that you will not get out until you pay the last penny. That's how serious anger is.

So what do we do? We've all had this cup of wrath at some point in our lives—if not so that others can see it, then in our hearts. We were fuming, scheming, steaming mad, drinking our bubbling, exploding cup of wrath. So what do we do? We look to the garden of Gethsemane and find Jesus there with another cup. As he is facing his death on the cross, he prays, "My Father, if it be possible, let this cup pass from me; nevertheless, not as I will, but as you will" (Matt. 26:39). What's the cup? It's not the cup of our wrath but of

God's wrath for sinners like us. It's his righteous, perfect anger directed toward people like us, who have so often displayed such unrighteous, unholy anger. And Jesus says, "If this is the only way, Father. I'll take it." We deserve that cup, but he took it upon himself. The only one who never violated any of the commandments or committed murder in the least degree in his heart was murdered for angry murderers like us. We have all poured out the cup of wrath on one another, but only Jesus drank from that cup for us.

7

An Affair of the Heart

You shall not commit adultery.

Exodus 20:14

As a part of my doctoral work on John Witherspoon, I had to spend time in Edinburgh at the National Archives of Scotland. I spent weeks looking at historical church records from the eighteenth century. It may not sound like a barrel of monkeys, but for this Presbyterian pastor it was fascinating to look through old minutes from various sessions, presbyteries, synods, and assemblies. Sure, there were technical debates, examinations, and minutiae that only historians would enjoy, but at the local church level, the issues were surprisingly relevant. In fact, most of the session records (think elder meeting minutes) dealt with sex and marriage.

For example, a woman named Margaret Snodgrass was called before the elders at John Witherspoon's church in Beith, Scotland, on September 25, 1747. She was asked if she was with child and responded that she was, though she was not married. She claimed that the father was one John Sheddan of Cuff. In the next month, the elders brought John before them and asked if he had had "any carnal dealings with Margaret." He vigorously denied the charge. The session continued to work with him, and he continued to plead his innocence, even though records suggest he was lying. Three years later, the issue was still unresolved. Margaret and John were now married, but they had been found guilty (again) of "uncleanness" and had to appear this time before the whole congregation.

Or consider another controversy that surfaced at that same church in 1747. William Mitchell and Elizabeth Cochran were rebuked by Witherspoon for their "irregular marriage." This was a common problem in eighteenth-century Scotland. A couple would clandestinely commit themselves to one another without the approval of their parents and without the blessing and formal ceremony of the church. They would get married in secret and then feel free to engage in sexual intercourse. What was the church to do? Were they married or not? Were they living in sin? For their part, William and Elizabeth were fined by the church.

Then there was the case of a man named George King and his servant girl Margaret. Margaret accused her master of committing adultery with her and fathering her child. George denied the accusations, claiming that Margaret was a loose woman who slept around. But the elders didn't believe George. When George continued to rebuff the session's efforts to bring the sin to light, they brought the matter to the presbytery, who also disbelieved George's profession of innocence. The presbytery said that George was "guilty of gross prevarication of such indecent behavior that he deserves to be publicly rebuked." And yet he continued to maintain his innocence. This lasted a full decade until George finally admitted, just as Witherspoon was leaving the church, that he was guilty of adultery.

Some things, and some sins, never change. In fact, scholars from other periods have found the same patterns. In his excellent book *Calvin's Company of Pastors*, Scott Manetsch examines the consistory minutes from Geneva in the years 1542–1609. During these six and a half decades, there were 1,572 disciplinary cases involving men and 777 involving women who were suspended for "quarrels," a catchall term for marital difficulties, abuse, or mistreatment. He found 636 men and 538 women who were suspended for fornication or adultery. Over twenty different offenses were subject to discipline during those years in Geneva, and the top two (by a wide margin) were household conflict and sexual sin.[1] Although we may have more access to sexual sin in our day, and a number of these sins are more socially acceptable now than they were four hundred years ago, it's still important to realize that at no age in the history of the church (or of the world, for that matter) have human beings excelled at controlling their sexual desires. Human beings then were like human beings now, with the same temptations and the same sin natures.

In my fifteen years of pastoral ministry, about 90 percent of the really difficult sin issues that come before the elders have had to do with sex and marriage. That's the way it has always been, and probably the way it always will be. This makes sense, since sex and marriage are two of God's greatest gifts. No relationship can be as intimate, sweet, life giving, and joy filled as the marital relationship, and no experience can be as intimate and powerful within that marriage relationship as sex. So, of course, the Devil is going to go after sex and marriage. We should expect confusion, misunderstanding, perversion, and pain—not because sex and marriage are bad or not worth the trouble, but precisely because they are such good gifts. God's best gifts are the ones most apt to be twisted and perverted by the world, the flesh, and the Devil.

There is so much we can talk about under the broad category of the seventh commandment, but let's limit ourselves to three sets of threes: three building blocks in the biblical definition of marriage, three Greek words that demonstrate the wide range of application for the seventh commandment, and, finally, three types of people who may be reading this chapter.

Forming a Biblical Understanding of Marriage

Let's start, then, by looking at three passages that are essential in forming a biblical understanding of marriage. Not surprisingly, we begin with Genesis 2:

> Then the LORD God said, "It is not good that the man should be alone; I will make him a helper fit for him." Now out of the ground the LORD God had formed every beast of the field and every bird of the heavens and brought them to the man to see what he would call them. And whatever the man called every living creature, that was its name. The man gave names to all livestock and to the birds of the heavens and to every beast of the field. But for Adam there was not found a helper fit for him. So the LORD God caused a deep sleep to fall upon the man, and while he slept took one of his ribs and closed up its place with flesh. And the rib that the LORD God had taken from the man he made into a woman and brought her to the man. Then the man said, "This at last is bone of my bones and flesh of my flesh; she shall be called Woman, because she was taken out of Man." Therefore a man shall leave his father and his mother and hold fast to his wife, and they shall become one flesh. And the man and his wife were both naked and were not ashamed. (vv. 18–25)

Our first building block is *complementarity*. God created marriage in such a way that a man and a woman uniquely fit together as complements, each for the other. We see this in verse 18: "I will make him a helper fit for him." And again in verse 20: Adam looked around, and there were birds, animals, and livestock, but "there was not found a helper fit for him." At this point, no one in all creation was a suitable complement for Adam.

So what did God do? He didn't create another animal or another Adam. He created woman. We see in verses 21–22 that woman was taken from man and given a name in relationship to man. She was "called Woman [*ishshah*], because she was taken out of Man [*ish*]." There is complementarity in how the woman was formed, in the name she was given, and in how she alone is considered a suitable helpmate for the man.

When man and woman come together in this one-flesh relationship in the context of marriage, it's not only a union but a kind of reunion. Adam and Eve, as *ish* and *ishshah*, were literally made for each other. Only through this understanding of complementarity does monogamy have any coherent moral logic. People like to say: "Marriage can be any arrangement of two people who commit to love each other exclusively." But why two? Why exclusivity? If loving commitment is the *sina qua non* of marriage, why limit the arrangement to a monogamous pair? The only consistent moral logic that demands monogamy and exclusivity is found in the Genesis account of a complementary pair—one woman uniquely fit for one man.

We see this same dynamic at work earlier in Genesis when God decrees that his image bearers should "be fruitful and multiply and fill the earth and subdue it" (Gen. 1:28a).

If God had created another man to be with Adam, or another woman to be with Eve, they would not have fit together because they would have been unable to fulfill this mandate. Only a man and a woman can be fruitful and multiply. Only with an understanding of sexual complementarity does the storyline of Genesis 1 and 2 make sense.

The second passage we want to look at it in forming a biblical understanding of marriage comes from the prophet Malachi:

> And this second thing you do. You cover the LORD's altar with tears, with weeping and groaning because he no longer regards the offering or accepts it with favor from your hand. But you say, "Why does he not?" Because the LORD was witness between you and the wife of your youth, to whom you have been faithless, though she is your companion and your wife by covenant. Did he not make them one, with a portion of the Spirit in their union? And what was the one God seeking? Godly offspring. So guard yourselves in your spirit, and let none of you be faithless to the wife of your youth. (Mal. 2:13–15)

If the word from Genesis was complementarity, the word from Malachi is *kids* (or "children," if you prefer the alliteration to line up with the same letter instead of the same sound). In verse 14, the marriage relationship is described as a covenant bond between two parties. With marriage, there are two things that constitute and ratify that covenant. There is a verbal oath and a ratification sign. The verbal oath is the solemn promise, the vows they made (and we make) "before God and before these witnesses." The ratification oath is the sexual act. Since the sexual act is meant to be private, a husband will kiss his wife during the wedding ceremony as a stand-in for the official oath itself. But make no mistake: the act of sexual consummation signs and seals the covenant.

From this covenantal union, and the accompanying ratification oath, God expects progeny. The translation of verse 15 is very difficult, but the ESV translation, which we are using here, gives us the gist: God seeks godly offspring from the one-flesh union of husband and wife. The language of making them one is a deliberate echo of the creation account. God designed marriage to be the kind of relationship that results biologically in new life (i.e., one that is fruitful and multiplies). While it would be wrong to say that procreation is the sole purpose of marriage, or that sexual intimacy is given only as a means to a reproductive end, it would also be wrong to think that marriage can be properly defined without any reference to the offspring that normally result from the one-flesh union of a husband and a wife. That's what God is seeking. By definition, marriage is the sort of union from which children can be conceived.

This means that marriage—by nature, design, and aim—is a covenant between two persons whose one-flesh commitment is the type of union that produces offspring. I know that because of medical difficulties or old age, this aim is sometimes not able to be achieved. But when a man and a woman are joined, it is still in the sort of union that is meant to produce offspring. In other words, we see from Malachi that marriage is oriented toward the rearing of children. That's the whole reason that the state has an interest in regulating and promoting marriage: marriage is oriented toward the rearing of children, and it's advantageous for the flourishing of any society that, wherever possible, the biological father and mother raise the children that come from their union.

Let me give you one last passage:

> Wives, submit to your own husbands, as to the Lord. For the husband is the head of the wife even as Christ is the head of the church, his body, and is himself its Savior. Now as the church submits to Christ, so also wives should submit in everything to their husbands. Husbands, love your wives, as Christ loved the church and gave himself up for her. . . . "Therefore a man shall leave his father and mother and hold fast to his wife, and the two shall become one flesh." This mystery is profound, and I am saying that it refers to Christ and the church. (Eph. 5:22–25, 31–32)

The relationship between *Christ and the church* is a paradigm for the relationship between a husband and a wife. The mystery is that the union of Christ and the church finds expression in a man and a woman becoming one flesh in Christian marriage. God designed for a Christian husband and wife to come together in such a way that this union of Christ and the church can be symbolized.

Notice that Paul's reference to the mystery of Christ and the church only works if there is differentiation in the marital union. Sometimes people get slippery with their language and say, "Yes, isn't it beautiful? With Christ and the church, you have this mutual indwelling, love, and support for one another. Any two people coming together can show that love and support for one another." But that's not the argument Paul makes. His argument is based on differentiation: namely, the man loves, leads, and sacrifices as Christ; and the woman submits and respects as the church. Paul did not foresee two individuals of any sex acting as Christ and the church, but rather that the husband would cherish like Christ and the wife would submit like the church.

We cannot insert two men or two women into the logic of Ephesians 5 and get the same mystery, let alone the same full-orbed picture of the gospel. That is why it's not a rhetorical exaggeration to say that the gospel itself is at stake in our definition of marriage. Paul himself links the gospel of Christ and the church to the expression of a godly Christian marriage, which can find fulfillment only in a husband and wife coming together in this differentiated union.

This is what a biblical understanding of marriage looks like: a relationship of sexual complementarity, the kind which (if all the "plumbing" is functioning) can produce children, a husband and wife showing forth the mystery of Christ and the church. Once you have these building blocks in place, the seventh commandment makes sense as something more than divine fiat. There is an internal moral logic that renders every kind of adultery, fornication, bestiality, homosexuality, and prostitution a violation of the divine design.

Three Passages That Show the Range of Applications

The seventh commandment, then, is about much more than a few sexual peccadillos. It's about safeguarding the gift of marriage and promoting the flourishing of the family. In other words, the seventh commandment forbids more than just cheating on your spouse. We can see that from the overview above and from three Greek words in a handful of New Testament passages.

Porneia. Jesus says that "out of the heart of man, come evil thoughts, sexual immorality, theft, murder, adultery, coveting, wickedness, deceit, sensuality, envy, slander, pride, foolishness. All these evil things come from within, and they defile a person" (Mark 7:21–23). The phrase "sexual immorality" translates the Greek word *porneia*, from which we get the English word "pornography." The leading New Testament lexicon defines *porneia* as "unlawful sexual intercourse, prostitution, unchastity, fornication."[2] Similarly, the New Testament scholar James Edwards states that *porneia* "can be found in Greek literature with reference to a variety of illicit sexual practices, including adultery, fornication, prostitution, and homosexuality. In the Old Testament it occurs for any sexual practice outside marriage between a man and a woman that is prohibited by the Torah."[3]

So *porneia* was a broad term, referring to any sexual sin prohibited by the law of Moses. In condemning "sexual immorality" Jesus was forbidding every kind of deviation from the created order. It's simply not accurate to say that Jesus never said anything about homosexuality or other contemporary controversies, because *porneia* would have covered much more than marital infidelity. Like all first-century Jews, Jesus would have understood that the seventh commandment covered a multitude of sexual sins.

Arsenokoitais. This is an important word, one that was apparently coined by the apostle Paul. Look at how the word is used in 1 Timothy:

> Now we know that the law is good, if one uses it lawfully, understanding this, that the law is not laid down for the just but for the lawless and disobedient, for the ungodly and sinners, for the unholy and profane, for those who strike their fathers and mothers, for murderers, the sexually immoral, men who practice homosexuality, enslavers, liars, perjurers, and whatever else is contrary to sound doctrine, in accordance with the gospel of the glory of the blessed God with which I have been entrusted. (1 Tim. 1:8–11)

Notice how Paul is running through the second table of the law, the last six commandments dealing with our horizontal relationships with one another. After talking broadly about disobedience, Paul moves in verse 9 to reference the fifth commandment ("for those who strike their fathers and mothers"), then the sixth commandment ("for murderers"), and then the seventh commandment, with two different phrases: "the sexually immoral" and "men who practice homosexuality." The eighth commandment ("enslavers") and the ninth commandment ("liars, perjurers") round out the specific commandments on the list.

Let's look more closely at the two phrases included under the seventh commandment. The phrase "sexual immorality" translates the Greek word *pornois*, related to the word *porneia* that we've already examined. The phrase "men who practice homosexuality" is also only one word in Greek: *arsenokoitais.* The first time we see this word in Greek literature is when Paul uses it in 1 Corinthians 6, and then here again in 1 Timothy 1. The word refers to something broader than the man-boy love (pederasty) that was common in the ancient world. Paul would have used the word *paiderastes* if that's all he had in mind. Instead, he coins this term *arsenokoitais*, combining the word man (*arsen*) with the word bed (*koite*) in a deliberate echo of Leviticus 18:22 and 20:13. The Septuagint (Greek) translation of the Hebrew in Leviticus 20:13 reads *hos an koimethe meta arsenos koiten gynaikos* ("whoever shall lie with a male as with a woman").

Even if you don't know any Greek, you can see where Paul came up with this new word. He employs *arsenokoitais* not simply to condemn man-boy love (though that was also wrong), but to express a blanket disapproval of all same-sex sexual activity. And remember, all of this is in the context of running through the second table of the law in 1 Timothy. In short, the New Testament explicitly treats homosexual practice as a violation of the seventh commandment.[4]

Epithumeo. The last word comes from the Sermon on the Mount:

> You have heard that it was said, "You shall not commit adultery." But I say to you that everyone who looks at a woman with lustful intent has already committed adultery with her in his heart. If your right eye causes you to sin, tear it out and throw it away. For it is better that you lose one of your members than that your whole body be thrown into hell. And if your right hand causes you to sin, cut it off and throw it away. For it is better that you lose one of your members than that your whole body go into hell. (Matt. 5:27–30)

The phrase "with lustful intent" (v. 28) translates the Greek word *epithumeo*, which means to desire, to covet, or to long for. Noticing that someone of the opposite sex is pretty or handsome is not a sin. The sin is when this noticing becomes *epithumeo*—when the recognition becomes desire, coveting, lingering, and lust. Adultery, in other words, is a matter of the heart. Of course, it's not only that. Jesus isn't saying you can have sex with whomever you want as long as your heart is okay. He's saying that even if we don't commit the physical act with our sexual organs, we can still be guilty of sexual sin by means of our thoughts, our fantasies, our reading, our clicking, and our affections.

Clearly, the seventh commandment has a broad range of application. We should not just think: "Well, I have never committed adultery against my spouse." It encompasses sex before marriage, pornography, bestiality, sex between men or between women, marital infidelity, and lust of the heart. There isn't an adult reading this book who fully escapes Jesus's penetrating words. No one is good to go when it comes to the seventh commandment.

A Message to Three Groups of People

Having looked at three building blocks for a biblical understanding of marriage and three Greek words that demonstrate a broad application of the seventh commandment in the New Testament, I want to finish by addressing three groups of people who may be reading this chapter: the tempted, the wayward, and the brokenhearted.

And in addressing these three groups, I want to do something a little different—mainly quote Scripture. Now, I know what it's like to read a book and come to several biblical quotations. It's easy to skim through them or skip them altogether. We assume we know what the Bible already says and are eager to move on to the meat of the book we are reading. But don't be fooled: the Bible is the meat. We need to hear what God has to say about the commandments, especially this one that can be so controversial, so difficult, and so painful. Don't tune out, and don't turn the page. Listen again—or maybe for the first time—and let the breathed-out Word of God teach you, reprove you, correct you, and train you for righteousness.

First, let me speak to the tempted (or more precisely, let God speak to the tempted). I'm thinking of those who are right now feeling drawn to something illicit or pulled in the direction of something unnatural. Perhaps you've been considering this week how you deserve a little sexual indulgence. Maybe you've been dabbling, lingering, toying around with sin. Maybe you're feeling intrigued and enticed by the possibilities. Listen to God's Word:

> Therefore let anyone who thinks that he stands take heed lest he fall. No temptation has overtaken you that is not common to man. God is faithful, and he will not let you be tempted beyond your ability, but with the temptation he will also provide the way of escape, that you may be able to endure it. (1 Cor. 10:12–13)

> The steadfast love of the LORD never ceases;
>> his mercies never come to an end;
> they are new every morning;
>> great is your faithfulness.
> "The LORD is my portion," says my soul,
>> "therefore I will hope in him."
>
> The LORD is good to those who wait for him,
>> to the soul who seeks him.
> It is good that one should wait quietly
>> for the salvation of the LORD. (Lam. 3:22–26)

> Therefore he had to be made like his brothers in every respect, so that he might become a merciful and faithful high priest in the service of God, to make propitiation for the sins of the people. For because he himself has suffered when tempted, he is able to help those who are being tempted. (Heb. 2:17–18)

> But each person is tempted when he is lured and enticed by his own desire. Then desire when it has conceived gives

birth to sin, and sin when it is fully grown brings forth death. (James 1:14–15)

Friends, let us not wander down the path to the forbidden woman (or man):

Her speech is smoother than oil,
> but in the end she is bitter as wormwood. (Prov. 5:3–4)

Stay away from the adulterous woman and the seducing man. Keep far from them and do not go near the door of their house. Drink water from your own cisterns. Let your fountains be blessed, and rejoice in the wife or husband of your youth. Get drunk on that love, not on the forbidden wine of iniquity. Mark well your path, for the wicked will be led astray by his great folly (see vv. 8, 15–23).

Second, listen to the word of the Lord, all you who are wayward. I'm thinking now of the duplicitous and deceived, the double-minded man who thinks he can show up for an hour on Sunday and fool God in the process. Maybe you still know how to put on all the appearances of being a very lovely Christian. Maybe you are trying to get away with something. Or maybe you know that what you've been doing is wrong, and you just don't care anymore. Or maybe you've convinced yourself that God doesn't want you to be unhappy, and so your marriage is expendable, but your sexual expression is not. Here's what God has to say:

Do not be deceived: God is not mocked, for whatever one sows, that will he also reap. For the one who sows to his own flesh will from the flesh reap corruption, but the one who sows to the Spirit will from the Spirit reap eternal life. (Gal. 6:7–8)

Do you not know that your bodies are members of Christ? Shall I then take the members of Christ and make them members of a prostitute? Never! Or do you not know that he who is joined to a prostitute becomes one body with her? For, as it is written, "The two will become one flesh." But he who is joined to the Lord becomes one spirit with him. Flee from sexual immorality. Every other sin a person commits is outside the body, but the sexually immoral person sins against his own body. Or do you not know that your body is a temple of the Holy Spirit within you, whom you have from God? You are not your own, for you were bought with a price. So glorify God in your body. (1 Cor. 6:15–20)

But sexual immorality and all impurity or covetousness must not even be named among you, as is proper among saints. (Eph. 5:3)

If then you have been raised with Christ, seek the things that are above, where Christ is, seated at the right hand of God. Set your minds on things that are above, not on things that are on earth. For you have died, and your life is hidden with Christ in God. When Christ who is your life appears, then you also will appear with him in glory. Put to death therefore what is earthly in you: sexual immorality, impurity, passion, evil desire, and covetousness, which is idolatry. (Col. 3:1–5)

You adulterous people! Do you not know that friendship with the world is enmity with God? Therefore whoever wishes to be a friend of the world makes himself an enemy of God. Or do you suppose it is to no purpose that the Scripture says, "He yearns jealously over the spirit that he has made to dwell in us"? But he gives more grace. Therefore it says, "God opposes the proud but gives grace to the humble." Submit yourselves therefore to God. Resist the devil, and he will flee from you. Draw near to God, and he will draw near to you. Cleanse your hands, you sinners, and purify your hearts, you double-minded. Be wretched and mourn and weep. Let your laughter be turned to mourning and your joy to gloom. Humble yourselves before the Lord, and he will exalt you. (James 4:4–10)

For this is the will of God, your sanctification: that you abstain from sexual immorality; that each one of you know how to control his own body in holiness and honor, not in the passion of lust like the Gentiles who do not know God; that no one transgress and wrong his brother in this matter, because the Lord is an avenger in all these things, as we told you before-hand and solemnly warned you. For God has not called us for impurity, but in holiness. Therefore whoever disregards this, disregards not man but God, who gives his Holy Spirit to you. (1 Thess. 4:3–8)

Hear the word, wayward ones. Do not think you can be a friend of the world and a friend of God at the same time. A man cannot serve two masters. God is not looking to be an escort as you walk sin down the aisle.

Finally, a message to the brokenhearted, to those of you who have been reading this entire chapter well aware of your sin in the past, or even very much in the present. You hate what you've done. You hate what has become of your life and your patterns. Sometimes you feel like you hate yourself. God wants to speak to the contrite, the penitent, the ashamed, and the sorry—to all those who have humbled themselves and laid themselves prostrate at the foot of the cross.

Out of the depths I cry to you, O LORD!
    O Lord, hear my voice!
Let your ears be attentive
    to the voice of my pleas for mercy!

If you, O LORD, should mark iniquities,
    O Lord, who could stand?

But with you there is forgiveness,
> that you may be feared. (Ps. 130:1–4)

There is therefore now no condemnation for those who are in Christ Jesus. For the law of the Spirit of life has set you free in Christ Jesus from the law of sin and death. (Rom. 8:1–2)

If we say we have no sin, we deceive ourselves, and the truth is not in us. If we confess our sins, he is faithful and just to forgive us our sins and to cleanse us from all unrighteousness. (1 John 1:8–9)

Then he showed me Joshua the high priest standing before the angel of the LORD, and Satan standing at his right hand to accuse him. And the LORD said to Satan, "The LORD rebuke you, O Satan! The LORD who has chosen Jerusalem rebuke you! Is not this a brand plucked from the fire?" Now Joshua was standing before the angel, clothed with filthy garments. And the angel said to those who were standing before him, "Remove the filthy garments from him." And to him he said, "Behold, I have taken your iniquity away from you, and I will clothe you with pure vestments." (Zech. 3:1–4)

And then, in closing, hear the words from the most famous sermon ever preached:

Blessed are the poor in spirit, for theirs is the kingdom of heaven. Blessed are those who mourn, for they shall be comforted. Blessed are the meek, for they shall inherit the earth. Blessed are those who hunger and thirst for righteousness, for they shall be satisfied. Blessed are the merciful, for they shall receive mercy. Blessed are the pure in heart, for they shall see God. (Matt. 5:3–8)

The promise for the pure is nothing less than God himself. Repent, receive, open your eyes, and see.

8

Treasures in Heaven

You shall not steal.
Exodus 20:15

After finding ourselves deeply convicted by the earlier commandments, our initial approach to this one is, "Yes! Finally, we get some breathing room." In a survey taken by the Barna Group several years ago, 86 percent of adults claimed that they completely satisfied God's requirement of abstinence from stealing.[1] "You shall not steal" is a good word for thieves and robbers, we think, but doesn't have much to say to ordinary people.

God Forbid

The outline for this chapter is simple. I'm going to use two questions and answers from the Heidelberg Catechism. We'll spend most of our time on the first one.

Q. 110. What does God forbid in the eighth commandment?

A. He forbids not only outright theft and robbery, punishable by law. But in God's sight theft also includes cheating and swindling our neighbor by schemes made to appear legitimate, such as: inaccurate measurements of weight, size, or volume; fraudulent merchandising; counterfeit money; excessive interest; or any other means forbidden by God. In addition he forbids all greed and pointless squandering of his gifts.

Let's walk through the answer line by line.

The commandment forbids outright theft and robbery—taking what doesn't belong to you. We see this a number of times in the Bible: Rachel stole her father's household gods; Achan stole some devoted things after the fall of Jericho, leading to the people's defeat at Ai; and Ahab and Jezebel stole Naboth's vineyard. We understand that taking things that don't belong to us is wrong—whether through breaking and entering, robbery, shoplifting, or larceny (the unlawful taking of the personal property of a person or business). That's what this commandment forbids.

The eighth commandment also prohibits the unlawful taking of people. While the Bible doesn't do as much to outlaw every kind of slavery as we might want to see from our vantage point, slavery in the Bible was very different from the slavery that existed in the New World. The chattel slavery that existed in America was actually outlawed by the eighth commandment: "Whoever steals a man and sells him, and anyone found in possession of him, shall be put to death" (Ex. 21:16).

You may remember looking at 1 Timothy 1 in the last chapter. In it Paul sequentially lists the different expressions of the Ten Commandments, and after he goes through some prohibitions in the seventh commandment—sexual immorality and men who practice homosexuality—he calls out "enslavers." He applies the eighth commandment to those who take persons. The whole slavery system that existed in the New World worked by forcibly taking people from their homeland (although in some cases, they'd already been taken by people in that homeland, and then sold into slavery). It was a violation of the eighth commandment.

Gisbertus Voetius, a leading Dutch theologian of the seventeenth century, listed four examples of stealing people:[2]

1. Stealing children to enroll them in a monastery.
2. Stealing children to use them as beggars.
3. Stealing young girls, sometimes to marry them.
4. Slavery.

Remember, Israel had been freed from slavery. God wanted them to understand what it was to be a free people, so they were not to enslave each other again. Yes, foreign people were sometimes taken as spoils of war, and Israelites could put themselves into indentured servitude, but capturing people for slavery was always considered wrong—at least, it should have been, if they truly understood God's commandments.

So the eighth commandment forbids robbery of personal property and of persons. That much should be obvious. The catechism goes on to say, however, that "theft also includes cheating and swindling our neighbor by schemes made to appear legitimate." The catechism goes on to list a number of these schemes.

The first one is inaccurate measurements. The Bible has a lot to say about this issue. Put yourself in the mind-set of how business was transacted in the ancient world. This was one of the chief ways of perpetuating injustice. People used cheating scales, false measures, or false weights. It was a way of getting more out of the transaction than was deserved.

In reading through some commentaries, I was reminded of a Norman Rockwellesque painting by Leslie Thrasher from a 1936 issue of the *Saturday Evening Post*. The painting contains a nicely dressed woman and a butcher looking across a counter at each other, both smiling as if they're getting a very good deal. Some sort of animal (maybe a chicken) is on the balance. If you look carefully, you can see that the butcher is pressing his thumb down on the scale, and she is pressing her finger up on the bottom of the scale. Perhaps that is a good picture of Americana (at times). It would be considered a violation of the eighth commandment.

In our day, where most business transactions are not conducted with literal weights and balances, we still have many ways to achieve the same end: accounting scandals to deceive stockholders, embezzlement (stealing money from work or church coffers), swindling the poor (perhaps because they don't know their rights), or taking advantage of the poor because they don't have access to courts or understand what's legally required of them.

The catechism includes fraudulent merchandise—selling defective goods or services, or enticing people to buy something that is not good for them. Discernment can be difficult in our free-wheeling, sprawling economy. How do we treat advertising? Some of you may work in advertising or study advertising. It's certainly not wrong to market something—to want word to get out about your product or service, and to promote it in an attractive way. But if you work in advertising or marketing, you need to ask yourself, "Am I creating a desire for something unnecessary or unhelpful?" It comes down to treating people as we would want to be treated.

Perhaps a drug manufacturer wants to pull out all the stops to show off a new pill that relieves heartburn or lowers cholesterol. The company wants to make money. Almost everyone does. So they're going to buy ads for that drug on *Wheel of Fortune* or *Jeopardy!* or at the end of the nightly news. They'll give it some fancy name that means nothing. They'll picture people looking healthy as a result of taking the drug. They want to connect the pill to the need. But what if the manufacturer develops a diet pill, and to get you to buy it, the company works to make you feel unattractive and worthless? The manufacturer needs to strip away your dignity so you feel as if you couldn't possibly live a meaningful life without the diet pill. It's a fine line, isn't it?

The catechism also covers counterfeit money. This includes check fraud—intentionally bouncing checks here and there, knowing that you'll eventually be caught, but feeling that you'll be able to cover the costs when that time comes. It includes the empty promises that exist in casinos. Casinos don't produce new goods and services; they merely exchange money without creating a new product of value—except, perhaps, the experience. And that whole experience is predicated upon certain people losing money—lots and lots of money.

Then the catechism mentions "excessive interest." Throughout the Middle Ages, Christians were hesitant to charge any interest. "If you lend money to any of my people with you who is poor, you shall not be like a moneylender to him, and you shall not exact interest from him" (Ex. 22:25). What does that mean for Christians who work in financial services? Does it mean that all kinds of interest, in every occasion, are considered wrong?

I think that the catechism gets it right when it uses the phrase "excessive interest." In the New Testament, Jesus told the parable of the talents, and he encouraged putting money in the bank, where you can gain interest. It seems as if Jesus was not flat-out opposed to everything related to banking, finances, or interest. Exodus 22 was a prohibition especially against interest on those who had no other financial options but to borrow at an exorbitant rate of interest. The interest here in Exodus concerned loans of destitution, for people who had fallen upon hard times. They didn't have insurance or governmental social safety nets to buoy them. What could they do when their crops were wiped out, or when they had nothing to eat because of famine, or when a storm came through and blew over their homes or tents? At such times unscrupulous people would offer to get them back on their feet—

for a price. It's that kind of attitude condemned by God, who commands neighbor helping neighbor. When we talk about interest on capital investments, the approach is different. Calvin argued that the situation is also different when you loan to those who aren't destitute but are just looking to start a business or buy property.

But even if interest is appropriate in a free-market system, it must not be predatory. Calvin insisted that he set the interest rate in Geneva, because he believed that determining interest rates was a moral and theological issue. Try that as a political policy! When you see people who have come upon hard times and you think, "Here's an opportunity for me to get rich from their misfortune"—that is what the eighth commandment forbids. We are to think, "I have extra that I could loan them without interest so that they can get on their feet."

Finally, the catechism references "any other means forbidden by God." This covers the landscape, doesn't it? It covers cheating the state. You might wonder, "Well, what's the big deal about cheating the government?" They also have the right not to be robbed. Such theft might occur through frivolous lawsuits, which cost taxpayers money; through refusing to pay or cheating on your taxes; or perhaps through defaulting on a government loan—because it's just the government, after all!

What about cheating employees of their wages? The Old and New Testaments both speak often against this practice. "Behold, the wages of the laborers who mowed your fields, which you kept back by fraud, are crying out against you, and the cries of the harvesters have reached the ears of the Lord of hosts" (James 5:4). James points out one of the chief ways of perpetuating injustice back then. Landowners would hire day laborers to work in their fields or people to come work with the harvest for a season. The laborers would do the work, but then landowners would say, "I don't think that was up to snuff. You missed a spot, and I wasn't really happy about it. I saw you taking a break." Then they wouldn't pay the laborers, which amounted to fraud and deceit.

The eighth commandment also forbids expanding territory unrighteously, through war or deceit, as when Ahab and Jezebel stole Naboth's vineyard from him. Stealing by "political nobility" (or "nationalizing") was one of the things that the Reformers often spoke against. Bullinger (a second-generation Reformer) said, "Those who steal private property spend lives in prison; thieves who steal public property walk about arrayed in gold and purple."[3]

What about insurance fraud? When we bought our first home, we noticed that the roof was in bad shape, but we didn't think too much of it because everyone told us insurance would pay to fix it. Unfortunately, the people who owned the house had already reported it to their insurance, gotten their check, and pocketed the money without fixing a thing. We were stuck. We couldn't make an insurance claim. Thankfully, we had a generous church with several people who, unlike me, know how to fix things. They got a party of people together, went up on the roof, and replaced all the shingles for us.

There are other examples of theft too. What about plagiarism, stealing from someone else's paper or sermon? How about online piracy, stealing music, movies, or software? Did you know that the most pirated movie, when it came out around ten years ago, was *The Passion of the Christ*? Something's not right there.

Then the catechism says that God "forbids all greed and pointless squandering of his gifts." Oh, great. Here we go. We're all going to get it now. We may think, "I don't take things. I don't pocket things when I go to the store. I don't break and enter. All the modern ways and business transactions are a bit interesting, but I don't do that." But what if you think about greed? I would define greed as "stealing with the eyes of your heart." First Corinthians 6:10 says that the greedy will not inherit the kingdom of God.

One of my sons is a terrific saver. He never parts with his money. I have another son who is always looking for new things to buy. He came up with some good logic this week. He told his brother, "I think that you have a problem with the love of money. You don't see me ever having any money!" That's not exactly what's meant here. You can be full of greed because you spend money all the time or because you save money all the time.

The Bible warns us against thinking that life consists of one's possessions. Jesus met a man who was squabbling about his inheritance and said, "Teacher, tell my brother to divide the inheritance with me" (Luke 12:13). Here he had a chance to meet the Messiah, and what is it that he wanted him to do? He wanted Jesus to settle his family squabbles and make sure he got his money. Jesus said in response: "Take care, and be on your guard against all covetousness, for one's life does not consist in the abundance of his possessions" (v. 15). Greed is wrong and foolish. It hurts others.

Back in 2008, at the beginning of the Great Recession, during the burst of the housing bubble, I read several books that tried to explain what went wrong with our economy. The overwhelming sense I got from my reading was that many people and institutions were to blame. Authors talked about Alan Greenspan, the Fed, George W. Bush, Bill Clinton, Fannie Mae, Wall Street investment bankers, and rating agencies. Some of the reasons that the economy went south were by-products of policies that people didn't realize would cause that. But in many cases these effects should have been foreseen.

One book looked at the human element, not just in policies that may or may not have contributed to the Great Recession, but in the greedy decisions that many people made. There were predatory lenders who wrote mortgages because they could and collected fees from people who didn't really need to refinance.

They sold mortgages to a hungry market. Some even sold unhelpful products that put people into loans that they could pay in the short term but not in the long term. That may well have been a product of greed.

There were also predatory appraisers. Lenders need appraisers to place a high value on homes for which they hope to issue mortgages. Appraisers need the work that the lenders bring their way. The two groups were happy to help each other out in ways that sometimes hurt the consumer. Houses were appraised far too high, and the industry could justify it as long as prices kept going up. People tried to flip houses quickly. Meanwhile, builders were constructing at a record rate, thinking they could sell their houses at inflated prices. Eventually, everything caught up with the bubble, and it burst.

But it wasn't just bad people somewhere in corporate America. The recession was also the result of predatory borrowers—ordinary people. Many borrowers lied on their loan application. They lied about their income, their assets, their employment, their credit history, and whether they intended to live in the house they were purchasing. One economist observed that as many as 70 percent of mortgages that defaulted in the first year turned out to have false information on the original loan application.

Greed has consequences, and no one is immune from them. Give it enough time, and we will all face the temptation to put profit above people and principles, whether that's wasting your employer's time, slacking off, fudging expense reports, taking out of the warehouse, falsifying sign-in sheets, giving merchandise away, or swiping from the cash register.

My very first job was handling bottle returns third shift at a grocery store. I don't mean to be judgmental, but the people coming in with bags of beer bottles at three o'clock in the morning are sometimes a bit dicey. These were the days before automatic machines, so I had to sort everything by hand and print out a receipt for the deposit (ten cents for every can or bottle in Michigan). People would often state the number of bottles and then walk away with their money, leaving me to discover after the fact that the bag was full of rocks and stones. On the other side, I saw employees print off receipts for themselves at the end of their shifts. The whole place was such a stinky, disorganized mess that no one knew the difference.

The eighth commandment also forbids the sort of attitude that says, "Somebody else will take care of this and provide." As Paul instructed:

> Let the thief no longer steal, but rather let him labor, doing honest work with his own hands, so that he may have something to share with anyone in need. (Eph. 4:28)

> Aspire to live quietly, and to mind your own affairs, and to work with your hands, as we instructed you, so that you may walk properly before outsiders and be dependent on no one. (1 Thess. 4:11–12)

> For even when we were with you, we would give you this command: If anyone is not willing to work, let him not eat. (2 Thess. 3:10)

Surely we can be thankful for all the different avenues of help that come from individuals, charities, and organizations. Certainly there are many social and governmental programs that help people fill in the cracks. But that's not an excuse. In fact, the Bible warns against thinking, "Well, there will always be another check. The government has got trillions of dollars. The church has got thousands of dollars. What does it matter?" It's robbery, taking what doesn't belong to you when there is an opportunity to work and not waste, and it is forbidden in the eighth commandment.

God Require

Here's the second question I want us to look at from the Heidelberg Catechism:

Q. 111: What does God require of you in this commandment?

A: That I do whatever I can for my neighbor's good, that I treat others as I would like them to treat me, and that I work faithfully so that I may share with those in need.

The eighth commandment is not simply about refraining from stealing. You may think, "All I've got to do is just not take stuff. I'll try to work on my heart so that I'm not so greedy. Then I'm good. I'm not a net negative." But the eighth commandment requires more than that. It means thinking of others as we would want to be thought of:

"I want laws, virtues, and practices that protect and promote my neighbor's well-being."

"I want to work hard so that I may be able to help my neighbor when he is not doing well."

The commandment enjoins us not only to refrain from taking things but to have a spirit of generosity, so that we love to give things and help those in need.

The eighth commandment assumes the right to and goodness of private property. That's not just a modern idea. It's all through the Bible. Old Testament law operates under the assumption that God cares a lot about personal possessions. Why would he make one of the Ten Commandments about not stealing if there isn't something sacred about private property and personal possessions? Exodus 22 has a whole list of commands that have to do with boundary markers, setting apart one's property.

Even in Acts, the picture of the early church is one where people freely gave, shared, and provided for one another, but they did so by selling their possessions. They were not some sort of commune or communist society, where people just put all their possessions in a pot and nobody owned anything. It was a communal instinct. There's a big difference. They still owned things, but a spirit of generosity prompted them to share with any who were in need. They sold off their possessions so that they might help their brothers and sisters. The management of possessions was an individual matter, even as the concern was for the community first.

So possessions are not bad. We see in the Old Testament that national prosperity was chief among Israel's covenant blessings. Job gave to the poor and, at the same time, did not take offense when his children enjoyed feasts. Jesus encouraged his disciples to give up land, family, and possessions, because they would get even more in the age to come. He wasn't above motivating with the good of possessions and prosperity.

Certainly we should not take what does not belong to us. But by implication, it's important that we're allowed to keep and enjoy what does belong to us, that we might freely share it with others. We see it in Ephesians 4:28. We see it again in the catechism. Think about it. Some of you love your job, but others feel that their job is a soul-shriveling dead end. We could examine a whole theology of work, but one of the reasons that we are to work hard is to have something to share with others when they're in need.

I love this quote from R. Kent Hughes: "Every time I give, I declare that money does not control me. Perpetual generosity is a perpetual de-deification of money."[4] Where your treasure is, there your heart will be also. But the reverse is also true: where your treasure goes, your heart tends to follow. If you put all of your treasure into your stuff—your toys, your man cave, your exercise room, your car, or your house—then your heart is going to go there. If you're having a hard time getting your heart in the right place, then send your money ahead of it. Your heart will follow. When you give generously to the church and to other kingdom-minded causes and organizations, you start finding that your heart is interested in what is happening.

Some of us steal by robbing God. Malachi 3:1–12 warns against withholding the tithe. The prophet considers that to be robbery from God, because God is ultimately the owner of everything. Whatever we have is on loan from him. The eighth commandment is ultimately an injunction for all of us to be good stewards. We are caretakers, and we want to use our gifts and opportunities wisely (Matt. 25:14–30). We want to use our possessions to get people into heavenly places (see the parable of the dishonest manager in Luke 16:1–13) so that we store up treasures in heaven.

Have you ever noticed that Jesus is sometimes less "spiritual" than we might think? That doesn't sound right, but here's what I mean: we might think that Jesus would tell us, "Do you want possessions? Shame on you. Do you want security and safety? Shame on you. Why don't you desire something more important?" He doesn't do that, though. Instead, he taps into the desires of all human beings. We want to make sure that we have something that will last. We want to make sure that we have enough for the future. Jesus says, "Okay, I get that. Let me tell you how to really be happy: store up treasures in heaven!"

Jesus is never against the human impulse for treasure. He's against the fool who thinks that earthly treasure really satisfies or lasts. The old joke is that you never see a hearse pulling a U-Haul. You can't take it with you. Do you want to be safe and secure? Do you want to have enough? Do you want to have mansions and palaces? Do you want to rule? Do you want to have treasure that never rusts, stock that never depreciates, and a retirement account that never loses value? Good! Let me tell you how you can have it: store up treasure in heaven. There's no rust or moths there. There are no downturns in the economy there. Think about what really matters. The desire for security is not bad. The desire for possessions is not bad. The desire for joy is not bad. But Jesus says, "Don't be a fool about it."

Think of the astonishing promise Peter gives to us: "[God] has caused us to be born again to a living hope through the resurrection of Jesus Christ from the dead, to an inheritance that is imperishable, undefiled, and unfading, kept in heaven for you" (1 Pet. 1:3–4). Wouldn't it be exciting if you went to a financial seminar, and the guru said, "I can promise you a retirement account that will never perish, never be defiled, never fade, and never depreciate. Are you interested?" Yes! That's what the Bible says: "I've got that for you. It's kept in heaven for all who put their faith in Christ and walk with him in faith and repentance." We want to hold onto possessions and have something that nobody can take away, so Jesus says, "Store up treasure in heaven. You get the Holy Spirit as your down payment of this unimaginably rich inheritance to come."

Let me end with a piece of good news, lest you feel that the weight of the world is now on your shoulders. Now that we have focused on money, generosity, and greed, you might be wondering, "What good news is there for me?" If so, remember that Jesus breathed his last breath, died on the cross, and was crucified between two thieves—two absolute violators of the eighth commandment. They were robbers, bandits, rabble-rousers, brigands, thieves. But one turned to Jesus and said, "We are receiving the due reward of our deeds. . . . Jesus, remember me when you come into your kingdom" (Luke 23:41–42). And Jesus said to him, "Truly, I say to you, today you will be with me in paradise" (v. 43).

In that dying breath, he gave that man a promise of an inheritance that he had, perhaps, foolishly wasted his whole life trying to find. In that one moment, Jesus reoriented the thief on the cross, helping him see that only in God's Chosen One would he finally find what he was looking for.

9

True Witnesses

You shall not bear false witness against your neighbor.

Exodus 20:16

There's an interesting pattern throughout the first nine books of the Hebrew Bible. I'm not sure if the pattern is intentional or coincidental, or if you just begin to find these things if you look hard enough, but each of the books highlights one of the Ten Commandments through a particularly noteworthy case of disobedience—and it's done (almost) in the order of the commandments.[1]

Start with Genesis. Of course, at the very beginning of Genesis, Adam puts his wife, Eve, before God, and Eve puts the voice of the Serpent before God. This violates the very first commandment: "You shall have no other gods before me" (see Gen. 2:17). And the punishment for their violation was death—"in the day that you eat of it you shall surely die." So they were banished from the garden.

Then we come to Exodus. What's the most flagrant example of Israel's disobedience in Exodus? No doubt, the golden calf. And what happened when they violated the second commandment? God sent the Levites, who killed three thousand men; and he also sent a plague. So we see disobedience to a commandment, resulting in death.

Leviticus 24:10–16 tells of a man who blasphemed the name of the Lord, a violation of the third commandment. The punishment was death.

In Numbers 15:32–36 there's a story of a Sabbath-breaker who is executed for picking up sticks on the Sabbath. In the fourth book of the Bible, we see this egregious example of violating the fourth commandment.

In Deuteronomy 21:18–21 we hear of a rebellious son who dishonors his parent and is supposed to be put to death by the hands of the community.

When you come to Joshua, things are in a slightly different order. What's a particularly noteworthy sin in the book of Joshua? It's the sin of Achan. Lots of space is given to this incident. After the battle of Jericho, Achan stole some of the devoted things, a violation of the eighth commandment. The result was that he was put to death.

Judges is filled with lots of egregious sins, but the worst of them comes at the end, when the men abuse and murder the Levite's concubine. Afterward the Levite cut her up into twelve pieces and sent her to the twelve tribes, who said, "Such a thing has never happened or been seen from the day that the people of Israel came up out of the land of Egypt" (Judg. 19:30). The result is that they go to war with Gibeah (the clan) and Benjamin (the tribe), and slaughter their own countrymen. Again, a horrible sin. This time it's a violation of the sixth commandment, and the result is death.

From a chronological standpoint, we would expect Ruth to come next, but the Hebrew Bible has a different order than our

Old Testament. In the Hebrew Bible we go from Joshua to Judges, then to Samuel (1 and 2 Samuel together) and Kings (1 and 2 Kings together). The next book is Isaiah, and it goes into the prophets. So the first nine books give the history of Israel.

If you think of 1 and 2 Samuel, you may quickly remember the most heinous sin. It was David's adultery with Bathsheba, which violates the seventh commandment. The result is that his son dies, and bloodshed comes upon the house of David.

Finally, we come to the book of Kings. There are lots of sins there, but one particularly noteworthy account comes from 1 Kings 21:

> Now Naboth the Jezreelite had a vineyard in Jezreel, beside the palace of Ahab king of Samaria. And after this Ahab said to Naboth, "Give me your vineyard, that I may have it for a vegetable garden, because it is near my house, and I will give you a better vineyard for it; or, if it seems good to you, I will give you its value in money." (vv. 1–2)

Here we have the sins of bearing false witness and coveting. Naboth refused to turn over his vineyard, so Ahab went home and pouted about it. Then Ahab's wife, Jezebel, said to him, "Do you now govern Israel? Arise and eat bread and let your heart be cheerful; I will give you the vineyard of Naboth the Jezreelite" (v. 7). So they devised a plan. They threw a feast and put Naboth at the center of attention. Then, at just the right moment, a man on his left and another on his right stood up and bore false witness against him: "Naboth cursed God and the king" (v. 13) Since there were two witnesses, Naboth was put to death on the spot, and Ahab and Jezebel got to take the man's vineyard after all. The result was that Ahab and Jezebel were eventually put to death by the Lord (v. 19). Once again there was an extreme violation of the commandments, and the result was death.

We have this pattern in each of the first nine books of the Hebrew Bible—and, with the exception of Achan's sin of stealing—in order! I came across this pattern several years ago when reading a book on the subject, and it raises a few questions: Was this an intentional pattern? Did somebody organize the books this way later on? Was God's hand present in placing these stories just like this? Even if it's all a coincidence, it's still a striking display of how seriously God treats infractions of the Ten Commandments. In each book we have at least one flagrant example of disobedience, and in each case, it's met with death.

Can I Get a Witness?

We often think of the ninth commandment as "Do not lie," and that is the gist of it, but it's specifically put in the context of the courtroom. Witnesses were everything in the ancient world. They're important today, but we also have audio recordings, videos, fingerprints, and DNA testing. They didn't have any of that, but they had eyewitnesses. If someone stood up to accuse a person of wrongdoing, and a second person stood up with the same accusation, the life of the accused could be in jeopardy.

> On the evidence of two witnesses or of three witnesses the one who is to die shall be put to death; a person shall not be put to death on the evidence of one witness. (Deut. 17:6)

> These are the things that you shall do: Speak the truth to one another; render in your gates judgments that are true and make for peace. (Zech. 8:16)

> Do not admit a charge against an elder except on the evidence of two or three witnesses. (1 Tim. 5:19)

What we see throughout the Ten Commandments is that each commandment often gives us the worst example of sinning in some way. For instance, murder is the worst way of breaking the sixth commandment, but Jesus tells us that it's not the only way. You can also be angry. Adultery is the worst way of violating the seventh commandment, but Jesus tells us that if you lust after someone, you have also sinned. So, with the ninth commandment, the worst thing you can do is bear false witness in a court of law, where someone's life could be snuffed out because of your deceit.

The commandment doesn't cover just courtroom infractions. It deals with all manner of falsehoods. Throughout the Ten Commandments we've seen that God cares about justice. Why would he make laws against murder except that he cares about each person made in his image? Why would he make laws against stealing except that he cares about the right of private property? Here we see that God cares deeply about verbal justice. "Sticks and stones may break my bones, but words will never hurt me" just isn't true. Lies hurt people deeply. This command was meant to protect marriages, property, life, reputation, and honor.

We see lies in the Bible from start to finish. The Serpent was the first liar. Jacob lied. Laban lied. A lie led to Christ's crucifixion. Ananias and Sapphira told a little lie. They sold some property, and gave the proceeds to the church. What a nice thing to do! But they lied about how much they had given (see Acts 5:1–11). They had kept some for themselves, which they had a right to do, but they lied about it. I can just see it:

> "Oh, Ananias and Sapphira! You have a great love offering here for the end-of-Christmas celebration!"
>
> "Yes, we sold a property, and we've given it all to the church."

But they'd given only half to the church, so God struck them dead on the spot for lying to the Holy Spirit.

We treat our words so casually and carelessly. We make wedding vows, looking him or her in the eye, saying, "I will love, honor,

and cherish you until death do us part"—and then we find someone else. We get a little bored. We run into difficulty. Someone gets
sick. Then our words just fall away.

Never, Never

What is God after with the ninth commandment? Again, the Heidelberg Catechism gives a useful summary:

> That I never give false testimony against anyone, twist no
> one's words, not gossip or slander, nor join in condemning
> anyone rashly or without a hearing. Rather, in court and ev-
> erywhere else, I should avoid lying and deceit of every kind;
> these are the very devices the devil uses, and they would call
> down on me God's intense wrath. I should love the truth,
> speak it candidly, and openly acknowledge it. And I should do
> what I can to guard and advance my neighbor's good name.[2]

Think about each of those phrases. First, "never give false testi-
mony against anyone." The Hebrew language of the Old Testament had six different ways of saying "false witness," which occur
in some sixteen different passages. This is not a small theme in
the Bible.

Second, "twist no one's words." Isn't this easy to do? We don't
even have to try. We do it naturally. We know how to retell a story
so that we're the hero and others are the goat, where we empha-
size only the really mean thing they said to us but say nothing
about the hard and hurtful things we may have said. We're masters at passing along our interpretation of the events as if it were
factual. Whether we realize it or not, especially when we're engaged in some sort of conflict, we intuitively know how to pass
along information with a certain implied tone. We know how to
leave out information and summarize long conversations in a way
that makes us (or our side) look good and others (and their side)

look bad. Don't think that "spin" is just what famous people do. We all spin.

Third, the ninth commandment forbids "gossip or slander." Gossip is passing along a report or rumor that cannot be substantiated. But gossip is more than that. We also gossip when we pass along a true report unnecessarily. Some of you may think, "I don't pass along things I don't know—but, yeah, if I pass along that someone had slept with someone, or someone just got fired from a job, I'm not gossiping. I'm just telling people the truth." But you need to ask yourself: Is it necessary to pass along this information?

We all understand that there are gray areas. I face this all the time as a pastor: Is this something I should share with my wife? Is this something I should talk to the other elders about? You may have similar areas of discretion. But you need to ask yourself: Would the person I'm about to talk about be happy if I were to pass along this information? Now, if you pass along that he just graduated with honors, got a great new job, or won an award—yes, that's great. You can gossip good news. But would he be happy for this bit of bad news to be shared, even if it's true?

Or ask yourself, What am I going to do as a result of telling this third party about this other person? In my life, and probably in yours too, I've found, sadly, that it's easy to make an intimate relational connection over secrets. People love secrets—especially juicy, bad ones. There's no faster way to make a friend than to find a mutual enemy. So you begin talking about people. You're "only saying what is true," but is it necessary? What are you going to do after you've talked to this other person? Perhaps you're really seeking out council as to how you can best love the one you're talking about, or developing a plan of action to go and speak or confess to him or her. But when in doubt, keep the circle as small as possible.

It's wrong to gossip and wrong to listen to gossip. "The words of a whisperer are like delicious morsels; / they go down into the inner parts of the body" (Prov. 18:8). This is really difficult for us. Sometimes you have to stop and say, "Time out for a second. I'm not sure if we should be having this conversation right now. I don't mean to be critical, but I'm just not sure." Sometimes our silence in the face of gossip is as sinful as the gossip itself. We just listen and take it in, when instead we need to do the courageous thing and say, "You know what? I don't think we know all the facts. We need to stop right here."

While gossip is passing along what you may not know, or passing along what's true but unnecessary, slander goes one step further. It's deliberately passing along what is false. Jesus considered slander a serious sin: "For out of the heart come evil thoughts, murder, adultery, sexual immorality, theft, false witness, slander. These are what defile a person" (Matt. 15:19–20a). Sometimes we make mistakes and pass along information that proves inaccurate. But too often we are quick to pass along unsubstantiated, false reports. That's slander.

Slander also includes assuming the worst possible motives for other people's intentions and refusing to ever give people the benefit of the doubt. This happens all the time. Something happens to us, and we just assume, "She didn't talk to me because she's really mad at me," or, "The way he wrote that email—he must be thinking such and such." We develop elaborate hypotheses and speculations, and when we tell other people, we pass it along as truth:

> "Oh, man, she is so ticked off at me."
> "How do you know that?"
> "Well, she hasn't said she's mad, but it's the way she looked at me."

Time out. Are you giving a true witness to your friend, or your brother or sister?

Fourth, we should not "join in condemning anyone rashly or without a hearing." As Jesus said, "Judge not, that you be not judged" (Matt. 7:1). It's the one verse that everyone in our world knows, it seems. It's abused, and we get that. Jesus isn't saying that you have to turn off your brain—that you can't be a critical thinker or ever make evaluations of people or of situations. What he's saying is that the measure you use for others will be the measure used on you. If you jump to conclusions, form your opinions of people based on your first interaction, and reach conclusions without all the information, you can expect people to do the same to you. Paul warns against this kind of rash judgment: "Therefore do not pronounce judgment before the time, before the Lord comes, who will bring to light the things now hidden in darkness and will disclose the purposes of the heart. Then each one will receive his commendation from God" (1 Cor. 4:5).

One of the foundational points of Western jurisprudence is that you're innocent until proven guilty. It's a biblical idea. Proverbs says that we should hear both sides: "The one who states his case first seems right, / until the other comes and examines him" (Prov. 18:17). We should want to hear all the facts of the case before we come to a determination.

I have never been seated on a jury, but it seems that I get summoned for jury duty every few months. When you go to the courthouse, you sit in a room with seventy or eighty people as the lawyers try to figure out who among those prospective jurors will be the most fair and impartial. As the process gets underway, the judge often reminds people of the presumption of innocence. If the judge doesn't do it, a good defense attorney will. The defense attorney might ask, "What must I do for you to acquit my client of these allegations? What must I present before you in order for you to acquit him or her? The answer is: nothing. According to the law, this person is presumed innocent until proven guilty, so I don't

149

need to do anything. Instead, the prosecution needs to prove that this person is guilty."

Presuming innocence doesn't mean that we never make judgments or that we aren't critical thinkers, but it does mean that we withhold a final verdict until we have as much information as we can. We don't make judgments without cause, and we hope that people end up being better than we think.

This is a huge challenge in our day of social media and trial by Twitter. The pattern is predictable. It happens all the time, and it's always sad and difficult. Some serious allegation is made against some person of notoriety or infamy—maybe a pastor, a doctor, a politician, a black man, or a police officer. Sometimes the charge seems credible; other times it seems like speculation and gossip. Either way, across the spectrum, trial by Twitter will ensue, and people demand that others take a side and jump into the fray. If you don't, you're likely to be accused yourself: "Why don't you say something? How can you be silent now, in the midst of all these allegations? Shame on you!" If you don't participate, you're accused of not believing the victims or of not caring about justice.

This is a challenge for anyone to navigate, because if the allegations are proven true, it's terrible, tragic, sad, and even horrendous at times. But if they're proven false or misleading, it's often too late to save the reputation or even the life of the accused.

We must not condemn anyone without a hearing or without just cause, and that means that we must do the difficult, unpopular thing of saying, "Hold on. I know the situation looks bad, but let's hold off until we have more information." Courts can make unjust decisions. Church courts can make wrong decisions. We live in a fallen world. We must exercise patience! Don't condemn without a fair trial or hearing.

During the 1996 Summer Olympics, a pipe bomb was found in a nearby park, and a security guard, Richard Jewell, found the bomb and dispersed the crowd before any explosion occurred. He was credited with saving lives and was hailed as a hero. But as the FBI conducted an investigation, the hero became a prime suspect. On live television the FBI searched his mother's apartment, and they took away his pickup truck. It seemed for all the world that the hero was the one who actually committed the crime, but in time he was exonerated.

We make these sorts of judgments all the time.[3]

The Heidelberg Catechism adds this: "Rather, in court and everywhere else, I should avoid lying and deceit of every kind." It happens so quickly. Some reporter tweets out something negative about a noteworthy politician, pastor, or athlete, and it gets four thousand retweets. Later in the day there is a retraction, and the correction gets three hundred retweets. Bad news travels much faster than good news. We must be careful to avoid deceit of every kind, intentional or not.

Some of us are compulsive exaggerators. It seems like a little thing, but it's not. I find this temptation in my own heart on how far I ran, how many hours of sleep I got, how long it took me to shovel the snow, what sort of grades I got, what I ate, etc. Are you someone who can be trusted to represent yourself accurately in even the smallest details of your life? We must avoid making promises we cannot keep or do not intend to follow through on. "It is better that you should not vow than that you should vow and not pay" (Eccles. 5:5).

In short, we must do whatever we can to protect our neighbor's good name. "A good name is to be chosen rather than great riches, / and favor is better than silver or gold" (Prov. 22:1). Most of us could recover more quickly if we lost our home, our cars, or our bank accounts than if we lost our good name. If you lose your stuff, people feel sorry for you and rally around you: "Let me love you. Let me help you. I can find you a job." But if you lose your good name and reputation, nobody wants to touch you. A good name can take a lifetime to build and a single afternoon to lose. It takes just a few malicious people on the Internet and scores of other people who believe it, and you're done. Calvin puts it well:

> We delight in a certain poisoned sweetness experienced in ferreting out and in disclosing the evils of others. And let us not think it an adequate excuse if in many instances we are not lying. For he who does not allow a brother's name to be sullied by falsehood also wishes it to be kept unblemished as far as truth permits.[4]

The ninth commandment is about more than not lying. It is, as Jesus summarized, about loving your neighbor as yourself. If someone was twisting your words and sullying your reputation, wouldn't you want someone else to say, "Hold on a second. I know him. I'm not sure if you have all the facts right"? Or, "I know her. Let me give you a different perspective here." Wouldn't you want a neighbor to defend your reputation?

Bigger Than You Think

Why is telling the truth so important? It's important because it is the nature of God himself. "The Glory of Israel will not lie or have regret, for he is not a man, that he should have regret" (1 Sam. 15:29). What makes God *God* and not human? One answer is that he doesn't lie—ever. "Let God be true though every one were a liar" (Rom. 3:4). As Jesus said, "I am the way, and the truth, and the life" (John 14:6). It's the nature of God himself.

Conversely, what is the nature of the Devil? He's the father of lies. When you twist and deceive, you're doing the very work of the Devil. From the very beginning—"Did God actually say . . . ?" (Gen. 3:1)—he shows himself to be a deceiver. He doesn't use just bold-faced lies, but subtle half-truths and misleading statements. He presents the bait and hides the hook.

We live in a time when words constantly bombard us. We read them, hear them, see them, and discount them. But God invented words. He communicates by words. He not only hallows the whole sphere of language and communication, but he considers language to be, in some way, an extension of his character. What is it called when God comes to earth? John says it is the Word made flesh (See John 1:14). God is present where his Word is present. That's how important language, speech, and true statements are. To reflect the character of God, we must speak true words and take great pains to say the truth and nothing but the truth.

One of my favorite movies is *A Man for All Seasons*. It's the story of Thomas More's refusal to support the king's divorce, and more than that, More's refusal to violate his own principles. At the end of the film, More is betrayed by his onetime friend Richard Rich. Rich comes in as the final false witness, which will lead to the execution of Thomas More. He claims that he heard Thomas More speak against the king (when he hadn't). Then, as Rich leaves, More notices a chain of office around his neck. It's the red dragon of Wales. And then More says, in a justly famous line, "Why, Richard, it profits a man nothing to give his soul for the whole world—but for Wales?" No offense to any Welshmen, but it's a brilliant line that expresses the Devil's bargain we make every time we lie.

It's important to speak the truth as a witness. Christ was led to the cross because of false witnesses. Stephen was the first martyr in the church because of false witnesses.

> There are six things that the LORD hates,
>   seven that are an abomination to him:
> haughty eyes, a lying tongue,
>   and hands that shed innocent blood,
> a heart that devises wicked plans,
>   feet that make haste to run to evil,

> a false witness who breathes out lies,
>> and one who sows discord among brothers.
>>> (Prov. 6:16–19)

Have you ever noticed how often God claims to be his own true witness? In Hebrews, we read that he swears by himself that his promise is sure. Jesus claims that he does not need another witness, because the Father is his witness. In Revelation 1:5, Jesus himself is called a faithful witness. Jesus says the Spirit bears witness to him (John 15:26), and Paul says that the Spirit bears witness to our spirits that we are sons of God (Rom. 8:16).

In Acts 1:8 the disciples are told: "You will receive power when the Holy Spirit has come upon you, and you will be my witnesses in Jerusalem and in all Judea and Samaria, and to the end of the earth." There is almost nothing more important than living our lives as faithful witnesses. Our words must be trustworthy at all times—otherwise, how will people believe us when we want to give them the words of life? Why should they trust us to speak of eternal things if we cannot be trusted to speak of temporal things? The good news is that Christ is our witness against the Devil and that our summons is to be his true witness in the world.

10

The Rare Jewel of Christian Contentment

You shall not covet your neighbor's house; you shall not covet your neighbor's wife, or his male servant, or his female servant, or his ox, or his donkey, or anything that is your neighbor's.

Exodus 20:17

The words of the tenth commandment are familiar, but slow down and read them one more time:
"You shall not covet your neighbor's house . . ."

They sure have a lot of nice stuff.

I'm so tired of living in this neighborhood. We live in a dump. It must be nice to live somewhere so fancy and so well decorated. Why can't I have the HGTV house?

"... you shall not covet your neighbor's wife ..."

Wow, she sure is beautiful. Why couldn't my wife age like that?

I wish I had married someone like her. I'd be so much happier if I hadn't married my wife.

Look at her husband. He's always so friendly. He's good with the kids. He helps around the house. He fixes things, not just breaking them. Why am I stuck with my husband when there are other men out there?

"... or his male servant, or his female servant, or his ox, or his donkey ..."

Man, my car is a piece of junk.

It's not fair. All our friends take great vacations. They go to the Grand Canyon or Disney World. Some go to Hawaii or Europe! We're lucky if we can go to Grandma's.

Why am I stuck in this loser job?

I wish my kids were more like their kids.

Why do I have lame parents?

"... or anything that is your neighbor's."

I wish I could be smart like him.

My life would be so much better if I looked like her.

Why couldn't I get a normal family?

Why can't I run, jump, throw, or be as strong as my friends?

Why is everything in my life hard, when everything for everyone else is so easy?

There's nothing necessarily wrong with noticing what other people have, but most of us don't stop and notice so that we can give thanks to God for his blessings to others. We notice and then stop being thankful for all that God has given to us.

A Serious Sin

The Bible speaks in strong terms against the sin of coveting:

> Since they did not see fit to acknowledge God, God gave them up to a debased mind to do what ought not to be done. They were filled with all manner of unrighteousness, evil, covetousness, malice. They are full of envy, murder, strife, deceit, maliciousness. They are gossips, slanderers, haters of God, insolent, haughty, boastful, inventors of evil, disobedient to parents, foolish, faithless, heartless, ruthless. (Rom. 1:28–31)

That's quite a nasty list, and right in the middle of it is covetousness. This is no sweet, safe, little sin. Paul makes the same point in Ephesians: "Sexual immorality and all impurity or covetousness must not even be named among you, as is proper among saints" (5:3). Even if covetousness here has sexual overtones, it's striking that the sin is named among those egregious sins that ought not be named among the saints!

So what exactly is coveting? For starters, it's not the same as having desires. The tenth commandment does not prohibit every kind of longing, want, or thought of having something nice or better. Jesus knew what it was to be hungry—to want food. While in the wilderness he knew what it was to be tempted. In Gethsemane he knew what it was to feel abandoned and alone. While on the cross he knew what it was to be thirsty. He knew what it was to suffer, and to ask God, "Is there some other way?" Yet in all this, he never broke the tenth commandment.

The law against coveting is not a law against feelings. In *The Rare Jewel of Christian Contentment*, Jeremiah Burroughs argues that contentment is *not* opposed to:

1. "A due sense of affliction."
2. "Making in an orderly manner our moan and complain to God, and to our friends."
3. "All lawful seeking for help in different circumstances, nor to endeavoring simply to be delivered out of present afflictions by the use of lawful means."[1]

Even the heart-searching Puritans didn't forbid weary Christians from offering a heavenward lament or saying, "God, I wish there were some other way."

The Bible often commends desire in its proper place. From Sarah and Hannah we see that the desire for children is a good desire. In the Song of Solomon we see that the desire for sexual intimacy is a good desire. The book of Proverbs encourages us to plan and to work hard so that we might improve our lot in life; so desiring some kind of domestic or financial advancement is not automatically wrong. Likewise, it's certainly not wrong to long for more of God or desire the outpouring of his Spirit. Those themes are present throughout the Psalms. Even Paul desired, in one sense, that he might die and go to be with Christ (Phil. 1:21). Clearly, the tenth commandment does not mean to make us unfeeling creatures without hopes or dreams or appropriate ambition.

That sort of thinking is more Buddhist than Christian. In Buddhism, the human predicament is caused by craving and desire. The Four Noble Truths state: (1) Life is suffering. (2) Suffering is caused by craving. (3) Nirvana is reached and suffering is ended when we stop craving. (4) Consequently, liberation is found in freedom from craving, which can be attained by following the Eightfold Path.

That's not Christianity. The Bible says our problem is not that we desire things but that we desire the wrong things or desire good things in the wrong way. As C. S. Lewis famously put it, the problem is not that we desire too much, but that we desire too little, "like an ignorant child who wants to go on making mud pies in a slum because he cannot imagine what is meant by the offer of a holiday at the sea. We are far too easily pleased."[2] We want fleeting worldly pleasures. But God doesn't say to us, "Shame on you for wanting things." He says, "I can give you something much better and more lasting than all the world's trivial trinkets."

Theft of the Heart

If coveting is not the desire itself, then what is it? What makes coveting such a serious sin? Let me suggest two answers to that question.

First, we covet when we want for ourselves what belongs to someone else. Coveting is more than thinking, "It'd be great to have a nice house," or "I'd like to have a better job." Coveting longs for someone else's stuff to be your stuff. Coveting says, "I want *their* house. I want *his* job. If only I could have what they have, then I'd be happy."

One way of looking at things is to see the tenth commandment as the internalization of the eighth commandment. Just as adultery of the heart is lust, and murder of the heart is hatred, so theft is the heart of covetousness. When Achan stole some of the devoted things from Ai, he first "coveted them" and then "took them" (Josh. 7:21). Likewise, James says, "You desire and do not have, so you murder. You covet and cannot obtain, so you fight and quarrel" (James 4:2–3). Those two sentences stand in parallel. Coveting is desiring something or someone that is not yours to have. Sex may be a good thing. Possessions may have their place. But they're both bad when the thoughts are illicit, when you want what does not belong to you.

Coveting is a violation of the second great commandment. Remember how Jesus summarized the two tables of the law: "You shall love the Lord your God with all your heart and with all your soul and with all your mind. This is the great and first commandment. And a second is like it: You shall love your neighbor as yourself" (Matt. 22:37–39). Coveting fails to love your neighbor as yourself. When we're covetous, we think only (or, at least, supremely) of what is good for us: what we would like, what would make us happy, and what could make our lives better, regardless of how others are affected.

It's easy for us to see how selfish children can be. They are happy with their Christmas presents until they see a sibling or friend get something bigger and better. Suddenly their Super Awesome Barbie Action Playhouse isn't so super awesome anymore. And you know what happens next? You'll hear those immortal words: "It's not fair!" This prompts one of the much-beloved mom or dad lectures about starving kids living in a crater on the moon. But as easily as we can see the selfishness of children, we can be blind to our own self-regard. We notice the camper down the street or the new addition with all the righteous indignation of kids on Christmas morning.

Coveting is not just saying, "I would like something." That can be fine. We all have wish lists. Coveting goes further and says, "Why did you get that? I wanted it! I am angry because you are happy, and I'd be happier if we could trade places." Coveting wants what other people have. That's the first way in which it's sinful.

An Expression of Discontentment

Second, we covet when our desire leads to, or is an expression of, discontentment. According to the Westminster Shorter Catechism, "The tenth commandment forbiddeth all discontentment with our own estate, envying or grieving at the good of our neighbor, and all inordinate motions and affections to anything that is his."[3] If the first point looked at coveting as a violation of the second table of the law, then the second point stresses how it also violates the first table of the law. When we covet, we don't believe that God is big enough to help us or good enough to care. Our discontentment is an expression of how much more we think God owes us.

There's a reason that "do not covet" is the last of the Ten Commandments. It comes at the end because it is such a fitting summary of everything that has come before. It's impossible to covet and love the Lord your God with all your heart and love your neighbor as yourself.

It can seem strange that the Ten Commandments start with such lofty ideals—"I am the LORD your God. . . . You shall have no other gods before me" (Ex. 20:2–3)—and then ends with a prosaic whimper: "Stop looking at that donkey." But do you see how the two are connected? God is saying, "I'm the only God you need. Don't turn to Baal. Don't turn to statues. And don't turn to animals or friends or abilities either. Let nothing else capture your gaze and affections ahead of me!"

Coveting is idolatry (Col. 3:5). It says I can't live without that person, place, or possession. It makes a god out of our desires. The tenth commandment is not anticlimactic afterthought. "Don't murder. Don't commit adultery. Don't steal. Don't lie. And try to be happy with what you have." The command not to covet is actually the practical summation and heart-level culmination of the other nine commandments.

Even though we understand from Jesus that the commandments all have an internal dimension, it would be easy to focus on mere external obedience if we didn't have the tenth commandment. When you look at the first nine commandments, they almost seem possible, at least in a perfunctory sort of way. "Don't kill people." I can do that. "Don't sleep around." I'm good. "Don't lie under oath." Got it. But just when we might be tempted to check off one commandment after another, we land on the tenth commandment and realize that we can't possibly keep this moral code to perfection. We can conceive of making it through life without a golden calf to worship, but no honest person can think of living out their days free from coveting.

I Saw the Signs

There are parallels to many of the commandments in the ancient world. Other nations and people had commandments against murder. Other legal codes tried to protect marriage, truth telling, and private property. But we've yet to find another law code from the ancient world that enshrines a prohibition against inordinate desires of the heart.

The tenth commandment makes explicit what the other commandments imply: obedience is a matter of the heart, which makes a proper diagnosis more difficult. How do you know if you're coveting? What does it look like? What are some of the outward manifestations of this inward condition of the heart? Let me suggest four signs that you (and I) have a problem with coveting.

1. You might be coveting if you've hurt others in order to get more for yourself. The hurting could involve actions, but more likely it will be done with words, attitudes, looks, sneers, sighs, and neglect. Do you have a "do whatever it takes to get ahead" attitude? "You have lived on the earth in luxury and in self-indulgence. You have fattened your hearts in a day of slaughter" (James 5:5). That's what James said in rebuking the greedy employers of his day who cheated the employees of their wages. It's amazing how God's people can convince themselves of compromise when money is on the line.

Have you started to cut corners where you wouldn't before? Maybe the little guy has been tripped up in your financial schemes (Ps. 10:2–3). Maybe in your rush to get ahead you've stirred up strife (Prov. 28:25). Or maybe your sin has been that of neglect. Your life has become cutthroat. It's all about the bottom line, with your family and friends getting nothing but leftovers. We may not mean to hurt them, but when covetousness grabs ahold of our hearts, sometimes we are the last to know.

2. *You might be coveting if you're preoccupied with making and accumulating more.* Are you like the thorny soil that started to bear fruit, only to have the seed choked out by the deceitfulness of riches and the worry of life? You get the picture from Jesus that these people didn't simply wake up one day and say, "From now on, it doesn't matter what I do. I'm going to cheat, lie, steal, and get my way to the top." They didn't make a conscious decision to turn from God. They just got too busy, too distracted, and too concerned about lesser matters.

That's the thing about possessions—the more you possess, the greater the danger that they start to possess you. Is it wrong to own a boat or a second home? Of course not. Many Christians use these things in a way that strengthens their souls and blesses others. But we have to be careful. What starts out as an honest form of recreation becomes a reason to be out of church and an excuse for dropping a missionary or two. Oftentimes, the sin is not the purchase of stuff but the time, energy, and effort required to maintain the stuff that shrivels the soul.

3. *You might be coveting if you're unwilling to give up what you already have.* Some people aren't interested in bigger and better. They just don't want to give up the safety and security of all they have. Again, the problem is not working hard, saving up, and being

responsible with our assets. There are plenty of proverbs to commend this behavior. The problem is when we hold on tightly to our stuff instead of letting some of the blessings of prosperity slip through our fingers and fall to others.

Think of the rich young man in the Gospels. He came to Jesus and asked, "What must I do to inherit eternal life?" He wanted to know what it looks like to be a good person. So Jesus rattled off the second table of the law—don't murder, honor your parents, don't steal—and the rich man said, "Great! I've done all those things." But have you ever noticed the one command Jesus left off? He didn't mention the tenth commandment. That is why Jesus added, "You lack one thing: go, sell all that you have and give to the poor, and you will have treasure in heaven" (Mark 10:21). Jesus knew that the man had a miserly heart bent toward coveting instead of generosity.

4. *You might be coveting if you're frequently grumbling about your house, your spouse, the quality or quantity of your possessions, and the general state of your life.* It's easy to think the next thing will finally make us happy. With two-day shipping, we hope that satisfaction is just an Amazon click away. It's always about the next thing and the next thing and the next thing. How much do we need? Just a little bit more.

Before officiating at a wedding I almost always pray with the bride and groom, asking that God would give them the rare gift of finding joy in the present moment. We're so often waiting for the next stage in life to be the one that makes our dreams come true. If only I had a girlfriend. If only we were engaged. If only the wedding were here. If only the reception were here. If only we were on the honeymoon. If only we had kids. If only we had a house. If only we had grandkids. If only we were retired. Contentment is dependent on the "if only," which, of course, is not real contentment.

The antidote to the sin of coveting is 1 Timothy 6:6: "Godliness with contentment is great gain." Do you see what the Bible does there? Coveting is about gaining. Isn't that why you covet? "I want to gain a possession, a friend, or a house." And God says, "Good! You want gain? I want you to have gain. I want you to have joy. I want to bless you. But you won't get it by coveting. You get it through contentment."

What do you love? What are you chasing? What do you think about in the shower, on your way to work, on the drive, or folding laundry? What is the one thing you think you need in order to be really, truly happy? If the answer is anything other than God, you're an idolater. God understands that our health and marriage matter; that we don't want to be alone; that family health and purity matter; and that we want peace, tranquility, relationships, a roof over our head, clothes on our back, and food to eat. He is not ignorant of those things, and he knows what we need.

Fill in the Blank

"If only I had _____, I would finally be happy." What's in that blank? A nicer house? A newer car? A spouse? Children? Grandchildren? Good looks? A successful career? Spotless health? For most of us, the blank is our functional god. That's the person, place, or thing we think we can't live without. Coveting, at its root, is idolatry.

When we covet, we are believing a lie about who God is and how he loves us. We must fight this temptation with faith. We must remember two things in particular.

First, we must remember how the story ends later. "He who loves money will not be satisfied with money, nor he who loves wealth with his income; this also is vanity" (Eccles. 5:10). Wealth will not make you happy. Asaph says in Psalm 73:

> As for me, my feet had almost stumbled,
>> my steps had nearly slipped.

> For I was envious of the arrogant
>> when I saw the prosperity of the wicked. (vv. 2–3)

Do you remember what turned his mind? He went into the sanctuary of God and discerned the end of the wicked (v. 17). He remembered the end of the story. He remembered what was coming later for the arrogant, the unrighteous, and later for God's people. "Seek first the kingdom of God and his righteousness, and all these things will be added to you" (Matt. 6:33).

And, second, we must remember who is with us now:

> Not that I am speaking of being in need, for I have learned in whatever situation I am to be content. I know how to be brought low, and I know how to abound. In any and every circumstance, I have learned the secret of facing plenty and hunger, abundance and need. I can do all things through him who strengthens me. (Phil. 4:11–13)

That doesn't mean that you can run a four-minute mile if you're a Christian, just by praying. It doesn't mean you can throw the football farther. It doesn't mean that you get the best job or the best grades because Christ is all. It means that God will be more than enough in your abundance and your adversity. Jesus said, "I am the bread of life; whoever comes to me shall not hunger, and whoever believes in me shall never thirst" (John 6:35).

We need to remember who is with us right now, the friend who sticks closer to us than a brother, the One who will never leave us or forsake us, the High Priest who loves to intercede for his people. He hasn't forgotten you. You aren't alone. How can you say you have nothing? You have him!

How do we begin to make progress in obeying the Ten Commandments? By turning to Christ, trusting that this Immanuel is the way, the truth, and the life; that he tells us the truth, so we listen to him and believe him; and that he is the only way to be forgiven, so that when we fall short of these commandments (and we will), we can run to him for mercy. We believe that he is the life, and that his commands are meant to give us life so that we may follow him and have an abundant life.

Epilogue

There are many ways in which I am not an exemplary husband, but one of the ways in which I am truly commendable is the number of Jane Austen movies I've watched. There was a new one that came out recently, called *Love and Friendship*. It was based on Jane Austen's little-known novella *Lady Susan*. The movie was quite clever. As with many of Austen's stories, this one had a lot of rich, foolish people. The star of the show, in my opinion, is the wealthy suitor, Sir James Martin, who is trying to woo the affections of Lady Susan's daughter. The actor who plays Martin does the part amazingly well.

In one scene, Martin is trying to impress all the people in the parlor with his knowledge of the Bible. "This reminded me of many such accounts one learns in childhood," he opines. "Perhaps the most significant in forming one's principles is that of the old prophet who came down from the mount bearing the Twelve Commandments, which our Lord has taught us to obey without fail."

There's a small murmur, and someone says, "Excuse me, I believe there were only ten."

Martin replies, "Really? Only ten must be obeyed? Excellent. Well, then, which two to take off? Perhaps the one about the Sabbath. I prefer to hunt. After that, it becomes tricky. Many of the 'Thou shalt nots'—don't murder, don't covet thy neighbor's house or wife—one simply wouldn't do anyway, because they are wrong, whether the Lord allows us to take them off or not."

The scene is hilarious, and the acting is superb. Besides that, Sir Martin's speech aptly summarizes how many of us think about the Ten Commandments. We've heard of them from somewhere, at some point in our lives, but we haven't dredged up the memory of them for some time. If we could, we'd like to drop a couple of them. And the others? Well, they seem like good commonsense notions, but most of us don't violate them anyway. So, once we've impressed our guests, we can go along our merry way. All in all, the Ten Commandments are a quaint relic to look at in a museum, but we'll be fine figuring out a moral code for our time right now.

Except that's not how God views the Ten Commandments. Not even close. He wrote the commandments in stone, by his own hand, and then ordered them to be secured in Israel's holiest artifact. And far from scrapping the Decalogue as yesterday's news, Jesus made a point to reaffirm the importance of the law and didn't hesitate to summarize our moral obligations, using the language of the Ten Commandments. Can we keep the commandments fully or perfectly? No. Do they serve to show us our sin and lead us to the cross? Absolutely. But the commandments also show us the way to live, the way to love our neighbor, and the way to love God with all our heart and soul.

We still need the Ten Words handed down at Sinai. Have they been changed in some respects by the coming of Christ? For sure—transformed but not trashed. We can no longer keep the Ten Commandments rightly unless we keep them in Christ, through Christ, and with a view to the all-surpassing greatness of Christ. As new creations in Christ, the law is not only our duty but also our delight. If we want to love Christ as he deserves and as he desires, we will keep his commandments (John 14:15). And that means as we keep in step with the Spirit (not to mention, keep in step with most of church history), we would do well to remember the Ten Commandments, which are foundational for all the others.

Acknowledgments

With any book there are always more people to write down and remember than can be properly thanked. But let me mention just a few. I'm grateful to University Reformed Church (East Lansing, MI) and Christ Covenant Church (Matthews, NC) who listened to (and hopefully benefited from) my sermon series through the Ten Commandments. The support and encouragement of both congregations has been life giving. My assistant, Kim Westbrook, helps me in hundreds of ways, including in the administrative details related to this book. Jennifer Dean, who also works in our homey church office, provided valuable proofreading and footnoting assistance. Andrew Wolgemuth was a constant source of support throughout the projects. As usual, Crossway has been great to work with. Special thanks to Justin Taylor for his friendship and encouragement and to Lydia Brownback for her editing skills. My wife, Trisha, is the best of the best. Every project could be dedicated to her, but instead I've dedicated this book to her parents, who are more than deserving as well.

Study Guide

Etched in Stone, Inscribed on Hearts

Introduction: The Good News of the Law

1. Review the "noncommandments," the moral code of our culture, on page 12. How do the noncommandments differ from the Ten Commandments, the moral code in God's Word?

2. Read Exodus 19–20. Why do these chapters in Exodus mark a high point in the life of Israel?

3. Why are we to understand the Ten Commandments as central to the ethics of the New Testament?

4. How is God revealed both in the giving of the Ten Commandments and in the content of the commandments? What application can we make from this revelation of God?

5. Kevin writes, "Freedom is enjoying the benefits of doing what we should" (p. 23). Explain what he means.

Chapter 1: God and God Alone

1. In what way is the first commandment foundational for all the other commandments?

2. How does the first commandment inform our worship? Consider Kevin's marriage analogy on page 33.

3. Review the nine reasons that Doug Stuart identifies for why Israel was drawn to idolatry. Where do you observe these occurring in the world around you? Which ones tend to tempt you?

4. How did the coming of Christ transform the first commandment? How do the following passages reveal this transformation?
   - Matthew 17:5

   - Philippians 2:10–11

- 1 Timothy 2:5

- Hebrews 1:3

5. How would you answer Kevin's four diagnostic questions on pages 38–39? How do your answers align with the four things we owe to God: adoration, trust, invocation, and thanksgiving?

Chapter 2: The Way of Worship

1. Read Acts 17:16–33 and answer the following questions:
   - What do you observe in the passage about the people of Athens?

   - How does Paul challenge their prevailing religious views?

- Where in the passage do you see violations of both the first and the second commandments?

2. Kevin writes that the second commandment forbids "self-willed worship" (p. 42). What is self-willed worship, and what is it not? How is the prohibition in the commandment demonstrated by the golden calf incident in Exodus 32?

3. How does Ezekiel 18:1–18 serve as a corrective to a wrong understanding of the threat given in the second commandment?

4. What five reasons does Kevin suggest for why God forbids images? Which one of these reasons impacts you most deeply?

5. Kevin identifies five ways that we can keep the second commandment. Which of these do you find most challenging personally?

Chapter 3: What's in a Name?

1. How does Leviticus 24:16 expose the serious nature of the third commandment? Why is the commandment so serious?

2. In what ways is the third commandment deeper than mere words? Be specific in your answer.

3. Read Exodus 3:1–15. What does this incident reveal about God, and how does it establish the significance of his name?

4. Kevin writes, "If we use the name of God to ascribe a false sense of authority to our ideas, plans, or opinions, we violate the third commandment" (p. 57). Can you identify a time when you have done this? Where do you observe this happening in the church today?

5. How should the third commandment inform our prayers? How about our worship?

Chapter 4: Rest, Rejoice, Repeat

1. In what ways has the Sabbath principle been observed since the time of creation?

2. The Gospels show us that Jesus never violated the fourth commandment. What were Jesus's activities on the Sabbath designed to accomplish?

3. B. B. Warfield writes, "Christ took the Sabbath into the grave with him and brought the Lord's Day out of the grave with him on the resurrection morn" (p. 71). How did this take shape during the first four centuries of the church?

4. How did Jesus fulfill the fourth commandment? What key Sabbath principles remain for us today?

5. How do you view Sundays? As you ponder this chapter on the fourth commandment, what changes might you make to how you live out that day each week?

Chapter 5: Honor to Whom Honor Is Due

1. In what way is the fifth commandment foundational to the second table of the law?

2. Read the law given in Deuteronomy 21:18–21 along with Jesus's parable in Luke 15:11–32. How does the contrast between the law and the parable reveal God's grace to us in Christ?

3. What is included in honoring our parents? What parameters must we use when determining how best to honor them?

4. How did Jesus demonstrate what it means to keep the fifth commandment? What challenges do you think he faced in the process and why?

5. In what specific ways does the fifth commandment go beyond simply the honor owed to parents?

Chapter 6: Murder, We Wrote

1. The sixth commandment is short: "You shall not murder" (Ex. 20:13). Despite its short length, it has lots of implications. Consider the following:

   • Where does killing in self-defense fit into the sixth commandment?

   • How does the sixth commandment inform our thinking about capital punishment?

- Has this chapter altered your convictions in any particular way?

2. How are we to best understand suicide from a biblical perspective? What comfort and hope does the gospel hold out to those who have lost a loved one to suicide?

3. Kevin recounts the final days of his grandfather, a time when his grandfather chose "to end treatment, not to end his life" (p. 102). Why was his choice not a violation of the sixth commandment?

4. How did Jesus transform the sixth commandment?

5. In what ways can we not escape the reality of our own guilt concerning the sixth commandment? What specific action of Jesus covers this particular guilt?

Chapter 7: An Affair of the Heart

1. Read Genesis 2:18–25; Malachi 2:13–15; and Ephesians 5:22–25, 31–32.

- How does the Genesis passage illustrate the principle of complementarity?

- Why is the sexual union between husband and wife an integral component of marriage?

- In what ways does the Ephesians passage show marriage as a symbol of Christ and the church?

2. Kevin writes, "The seventh commandment forbids more than just cheating on your spouse" (p. 115). In what specific ways is this true?

3. Explain Paul's use of the term *arsenokoitais*. How does this guide our thinking about homosexuality?

4. What does the Bible prescribe for dealing with temptations to sexual sin?

5. How can the sexually defiled be restored to spiritual purity?

Chapter 8: Treasures in Heaven

1. Question 110 of the Heidelberg Catechism asks, "What does God forbid in the eighth commandment?" The answer given is this:

    > He forbids not only outright theft and robbery, punishable by law. But in God's sight theft also includes cheating and swindling our neighbor by schemes made to appear legitimate, such as: inaccurate measurements of weight, size, or volume; fraudulent merchandising; counterfeit money; excessive interest; or any other means forbidden by God. In addition he forbids all greed and pointless squandering of his gifts.

    • How does the catechism enrich your understanding of the eighth commandment?

    • Is there anything here you hadn't considered before?

    • How might a deeper grasp of the eighth commandment change the ways you conduct yourself in business and in your personal life?

2. How does greed factor in as a violation of the eighth commandment? What do we learn about greed from the following passages?
    • Proverbs 15:27

- Luke 12:13–21

- 1 Corinthians 6:9–11

3. How does the eighth commandment serve as a guide for our personal relationships as well as for how we treat people in general?

4. Explain why Kevin writes, "Jesus is never against the human impulse for treasure" (p. 137).

5. Read Matthew 13:44–45.
   - How do these parables reshape your perspective on your material assets?

   - How can you cultivate this perspective in your own heart and life?

Chapter 9: True Witnesses

1. In what ways does the ninth commandment cover so much more than lying or bearing false witness in a court of law?

2. Kevin writes, "God cares deeply about verbal justice" (p. 145). Where and how is this illustrated for us in Scripture?

3. How is motive a factor in breaking or keeping the ninth commandment? Give some specific examples.

4. Proverbs 18:17 says:

   The one who states his case first seems right,
   until the other comes and examines him.

   • What does this mean?

   • Why do you think that failing to heed this wisdom is especially prominent in the world of social media?

5. From a biblical standpoint, why is telling the truth of such vital importance?

Chapter 10: The Rare Jewel of Christian Contentment

1. Define *coveting*. How does it differ from *desire*?

2. Explain the link between coveting and discontentment.

3. Why is coveting idolatrous? Where are you tempted to such idolatry in your own life? How can the following passages change the perspective of your heart?

   • Ecclesiastes 5:10

   • John 6:35

   • Philippians 4:11–13

   • 1 Timothy 6:6

4. Kevin writes, "The tenth commandment makes explicit what the other commandments imply" (p. 162). Explain what he means.

5. Consider the four signs (pp. 162–64) that indicate a problem with coveting. Which sign do you find most convicting and why?

Epilogue

Review Exodus 20:1–17 and then read Matthew 5–7, Jesus's Sermon on the Mount.

Identify all the places where Jesus references the Ten Commandments, either directly or indirectly. How does he build on the commandments originally given to Moses? What changes do you note?

Notes

Introduction: The Good News of Law

1. Daniel Burke, "Behold, Atheists' New Ten Commandments," CNN website, December 20, 2014, accessed September 21, 2107, http://www.cnn.com/2014/12/19/living/atheist-10-commandments/index.html. I first came across this story in John Dickson, *A Doubter's Guide to the Ten Commandments* (Grand Rapids, MI: Zondervan: 2016), 20–22.

2. Ibid.

3. "'Boaty McBoatface' Polar Ship Named after Attenborough," May 6, 2016, accessed September 20, 2017, http://www.bbc.com/news/uk-36225652.

4. "Americans Know Big Macs Better than Ten Commandments," October 12, 2007, accessed September 22, 2017, https://www.reuters.com/article/us-bible-commandments/americans-know-big-macs-better-than-ten-commandments-idUSN1223894020071012; Kenyon Cureton, "The Ten Commandments: Foundation of American Society," accessed September 22, 2017, http://www.frc.org/booklet/the-ten-commandments-foundation-of-american-society-.

5. "How Many Federal Laws Are There? No One Knows," February 7, 2013, accessed January 27, 2018, http://www.kowal.com/?q=How-Many-Federal-Laws-Are-There%3F,.

Chapter 1: God and God Alone

1. Tom Holland, "Why I Was Wrong about Christianity," *NewStatesman*, September 14, 2016, accessed September 29, 2017, https://www.newstatesman.com/politics/religion/2016/09/tom-holland-why-i-was-wrong-about-christianity.

2. Ibid.

3. Ibid.

4. Ibid.

5. John Dickson, *A Doubter's Guide to the Ten Commandments* (Grand Rapids, MI: Zondervan: 2016), 49.

6. John Calvin, *Institutes of the Christian Religion*, ed. John T. McNeill, trans. Ford Lewis Battles (Philadelphia: Westminster Press, 1960), 2.8.16.

7. Heidelberg Catechism, question and answer 95, in *Ecumenical Creeds and Reformed Confessions* (Grand Rapids, MI: Faith Alive, 1988).

8. Douglas K. Stuart, *Exodus*, New American Commentary (Nashville: B&H, 2006), 450–54.

9. Calvin, *Institutes of the Christian Religion*, 2.8.16.

Chapter 2: The Way of Worship

1. Westminster Larger Catechism, in *The Westminster Confession of Faith and Catechisms with Proof Texts* (Lawrenceville, GA: Christian Education & Publications Committee, 2007), n.p.

2. Westminster Confession of Faith, 21.1, in *The Westminster Confession of Faith and Catechisms with Proof Texts*.

3. Heidelberg Catechism, question and answer 96, in *Ecumenical Creeds and Reformed Confessions* (Grand Rapids, MI: Faith Alive, 1988).

Chapter 3: What's in a Name?

1. Act 2, scene 2. The entire play can be found at http://shakespeare.mit.edu/romeo_juliet/full.html.

2. Philip Graham Ryken, *Exodus: Saved for God's Glory*, Preaching the Word (Wheaton, IL: Crossway, 2005), 585.

Chapter 4: Rest, Rejoice, Repeat

1. Westminster Confession of Faith, 21.7, in *The Westminster Confession of Faith and Catechisms with Proof Texts* (Lawrenceville, GA: Christian Education & Publications Committee, 2007).

2. Ibid., 21.8.

3. Heidelberg Catechism, question and answer 103, in *Ecumenical Creeds and Reformed Confessions* (Grand Rapids, MI: Faith Alive, 1988).

4. *Reformed Confessions of the 16th and 17th Centuries in English Translation: Volume 2, 1552–1566*, comp. James T. Dennison Jr. (Grand Rapids, MI: Reformation Heritage, 2010).

5. Quoted in D. A. Carson, *From Sabbath to Lord's Day: A Biblical, Historical, and Theological Investigation* (Eugene, OR: Wipf & Stock, 1999), 314.

6. Quoted in J. Douma, *The Ten Commandments: Manual for the Christian Life*, trans. Nelson D. Kloosterman (Phillipsburg, NJ: P&R, 1996), 139.

7. Craig L. Blomberg, *Perspectives on the Sabbath: 4 Views* (Nashville: B&H, 2011), 311.

8. Quoted in Philip Graham Ryken, *Exodus: Saved for God's Glory*, Preaching the Word (Wheaton, IL: Crossway, 2005), 597.

9. John Calvin, *Institutes of the Christian Religion*, ed. John T. McNeill, trans. Ford Lewis Battles (Philadelphia: Westminster Press, 1960), 2.8.31.

10. Ibid.

11. Quoted in Carson, *From Sabbath to Lord's Day*, 327.

12. Quoted in Bruce A. Ray, *Celebrating the Sabbath: Finding Rest in a Restless World* (Phillipsburg, NJ: P&R, 2008), 115.

Chapter 5: Honor to Whom Honor Is Due

1. Quoted in Philip Graham Ryken, *Exodus: Saved for God's Glory*, Preaching the Word (Wheaton, IL: Crossway, 2005), 602.

2. John Calvin, *Institutes of the Christian Religion*, ed. John T. McNeill, trans. Ford Lewis Battles (Philadelphia: Westminster Press, 1960), 2.8.36.

3. Ibid.

4. Cecil Frances Alexander, "Once in Royal David's City," 1848.

Chapter 6: Murder, We Wrote

1. Julie Gossack, "Life after the Suicide of a Loved One," January 2, 2006; *Journal of Biblical Counseling*, vol. 24, no. 1 (Glenside, PA: Christian Counseling & Educational Foundation), n.p.

2. *Calvin's Commentary*, vol. 3, *Harmony of Exodus, Leviticus, Numbers, Deuteronomy* (repr. Grand Rapids, MI: Baker, 1993), n.p.

3. Edmund P. Clowney, *How Jesus Transforms the Ten Commandments* (Phillipsburg, NJ: P&R, 2007), 79.

4. David Powlison, *Good and Angry: Redeeming Anger, Irritation, Complaining, and Bitterness* (Greensboro, NC: New Growth Press, 2016), 23.

5. Heidelberg Catechism, question and answer 107, in *Ecumenical Creeds and Reformed Confessions* (Grand Rapids, MI: Faith Alive, 1988).

Chapter 7: An Affair of the Heart

1. Scott M. Manetsch, *Calvin's Company of Pastors: Pastoral Care and the Emerging Reformed Church, 1536–1609* (Oxford, UK: Oxford University Press, 2013), 181–220, esp. 201.

2. Walter Bauer, *A Greek-English Lexicon of the New Testament and Other Early Christian Literature*, 3rd ed., rev. and ed. Frederick William Danker (Chicago: University of Chicago Press, 2000), 854.

3. James R. Edwards, *The Gospel according to Mark*, Pillar New Testament Commentary (Grand Rapids, MI: Eerdmans, 2001), 213.

4. For more on this important word and the controversy surrounding it, see Kevin DeYoung, *What Does the Bible Really Teach about Homosexuality?* (Wheaton, IL: Crossway, 2015), 59–67.

Chapter 8: Treasures in Heaven

1. Quoted in Michael S. Horton, *The Law of Perfect Freedom: Relating to God and Others Through the Ten Commandments* (Chicago: Moody Press, 1993), 222.
2. J. Douma, *The Ten Commandments: Manual for the Christian Life*, trans. Nelson D. Kloosterman (Phillipsburg, NJ: P&R, 1996), 287.
3. Quoted in ibid., 290.
4. R. Kent Hughes, cited in Philip Graham Ryken, *Exodus: Saved for God's Glory*, Preaching the Word (Wheaton, IL: Crossway, 2005), 646.

Chapter 9: True Witnesses

1. This is the argument of David Noel Freedman in *The Nine Commandments: Uncovering the Hidden Pattern of Crime and Punishment in the Hebrew Bible* (New York: Random House, 2002).
2. Heidelberg Catechism, answer 112, in *Ecumenical Creeds and Reformed Confessions* (Grand Rapids, MI: Faith Alive, 1988).
3. For a documentary of the event, see "Judging Jewell," *30 for 30 Shorts*, season 1, episode 17, January 29, 2014. The documentary can be viewed at http://www.espn.com/video/clip?id=10365079.
4. John Calvin, *Institutes of the Christian Religion*, ed. John T. McNeill, trans. Ford Lewis Battles (Philadelphia: Westminster Press, 1960), 2.8.48.

Chapter 10: The Rare Jewel of Christian Contentment

1. Jeremiah Burroughs, *The Rare Jewel of Christian Contentment* (1648; Edinburgh: Banner of Truth, 2009), 21–22.
2. C. S. Lewis, *The Weight of Glory: And Other Addresses* (New York: HarperCollins, 1980), 26.
3. Westminster Shorter Catechism, question and answer 81, in *The Westminster Confession of Faith and Catechisms with Proof Texts* (Lawrenceville, GA: Christian Education & Publications Committee, 2007).

General Index

Scripture Index

ALSO AVAILABLE
from
KEVIN DEYOUNG

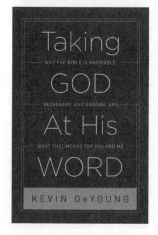